VGM Professional Careers Series

CAREERS
IN BUSINESS

LILA B. STAIR
DOROTHY DOMKOWSKI

VGM Career Horizons
a division of *NTC Publishing Group*
Lincolnwood, Illinois USA

Library of Congress Cataloging-in-Publication Data

Stair, Lila B.
    Careers in business / Lila B. Stair, Dorothy Domkowski.

        p.   cm. — (VGM professional careers series)
    Includes bibliographical references.
    ISBN 0-8442-8144-1   (hardbound)   : $16.95. — ISBN 0-8442-8146-8
    (softbound)   : $11.95
    1. Business—Vocational guidance—United States.   I. Domkowski,
    Dorothy.   II. Title.   III. Series.
    HF5382.5.U5S66   1989
    650′.023′73—dc20   91-18734
                                                                                 CIP

1996 Printing

Published by VGM Career Horizons, a division of NTC Publishing Group.
© 1992 by NTC Publishing Group, 4255 West Touhy Avenue,
Lincolnwood (Chicago), Illinois 60646-1975 U.S.A.

    4 5 6 7 8 9 BC 9 8 7 6 5 4 3

ABOUT THE AUTHORS

Lila B. Stair has an extensive background in career counseling and research. Her years as a career counselor involved both career decision-making activities as well as job development and placement. She has served as a counselor for Program for the Achievement of Competency Education (PACE), a consultant for a Washington state agency to computerize occupational services, and as a career counselor. She has also taught management and organizational behavior at Florida State University.

Ms. Stair is the author of several titles in the VGM Professional Careers series. She has an M.A. in counselor education from the University of New Orleans and an M.B.A. from Florida State University.

Dorothy Domkowski is director of the Student Aid Resource Center (STAR) at the Florida State University, Tallahassee, Florida. She has fifteen years of experience in the field of career development.

CONTENTS

JOB INDEX

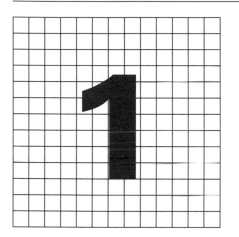

CAREER REALITIES: HOW TO ADAPT A CAREER DECISION-MAKING MODEL TO YOURSELF

CHAPTER OBJECTIVES

Upon completion of this chapter, you should be able to:

1. Describe the concepts "career" and "career development."
2. Discuss the nature of the entry-level position and career mobility.
3. List some economic factors likely to affect business careers today.
4. Relate the process of self-evaluation to a successful career.
5. Identify critical factors in career decision making.
6. Adapt an open career decision-making model to yourself.

A CAREER IS NOT JUST A JOB

The concept of a career implies much more than a specific job or the type of work that a person performs. Of the many definitions of *career*, the best for purposes of this book is the one developed by Doug Hall: "The career is the individually perceived sequence of attitudes and behaviors associated with work-related experiences and activities over the span of the person's life."[1]

A career spans an individual's entire working life and includes not only behaviors, but also attitudes toward work. A career develops in accordance with these attitudes and behaviors. In this sense, one does not select a career per se, but rather chooses first educational and work experiences in order to begin a career that develops from these experiences. For example, you may choose accounting as a field, major in it in college, and accept an entry-level position with a public accounting firm upon graduation. From that point, you may choose several paths along which your career will develop. You may start an independent practice, switch to private industry and ultimately become a chief executive of the company, or perhaps become fascinated with information systems and return to school for additional training in information processing. Figure 1-1 shows a sample career path of a college graduate. The choices are all yours!

---

[1]Douglas Hall, *Careers in Organizations* (Santa Monica, Calif.: Goodyear Publishing Co., 1976), p. 4.

Figure 1-1 Sample career path of a college graduate

THE NATURE OF THE ENTRY-LEVEL POSITION

As a college graduate, you are more likely to be hired for your potential contribution to the organization over time rather than for your immediate productive capabilities. The entry-level position is a testing ground of sorts. It is used by the organization to observe the level of competence of new employees in order to determine which of them possess the talent to assume supervisory and managerial responsibilities within the organization.

A story told by business professor Jack Wacker involves another business professor who enjoyed following up with his former students to see how their careers were progressing. One of his better students, in terms of academic ability and ambition, entered the sales force of a major national organization, a common position for a new graduate from the college of business. The professor ran into John, the former student, and asked how things were going after six months with the company. John answered, "Not very well."

Puzzled by this response, the professor spoke to John's supervisor. The supervisor indicated two problem areas: First, John's sales were considerably lower than the other new sales representatives, perhaps because he wasn't calling on enough potential new customers; Second, John's rapport with his coworkers was not particularly good, which limited the learning and growth on the job that usually result from association with other members of the sales force. After his talk with the supervisor, the professor shared these remarks with John over lunch.

Three months later, the professor visited the same company to do some consulting. He noticed the supervisor with whom he had spoken and asked about John's progress. The supervisor was obviously pleased with his performance and said that John had shown tremendous improvement over the past three months. In passing, the professor mentioned his luncheon conversation with John, at which point the supervisor accused angrily, "You cheated!"

How do you interpret that accusation? The point is that the supervisor expected John to have enough initiative to identify his problems for himself as well as to determine how to solve them. This is a type of testing of new employees that often goes on. Perhaps John was finding the college-to-work adjustment rather difficult. Or John's problem may have been that his expectations for employment exceeded his position in sales, and his disappointment may have been part of the reason for his poor initial performance. Still, this is the usual nature of entry-level positions.

From the organization's standpoint, the entry-level position normally is designed to smooth the transition from college to work, to orient the new employee to the organization and its values, and to open career paths within the company unavailable to the employee without the experience gained in the entry-level position. It is wise to be realistic about entry-level job experiences and to evaluate them as short-term objectives that help an individual reach long-term career goals.

A number of factors to which a new worker must adjust affect the nature of the entry-level job experience. The most important factor is the human organization and the new employee's ability to adapt to and work with it on an emotional level. For example, empire building, vested interests, and intolerance of innovation, particularly from new employees, may all contribute to undermining the rational efforts of the new employee to be productive. It is therefore necessary for the newcomer to learn to cope emotionally with first-job realities.

Understanding trends in the job market is particularly important for entry-level job seekers. Major transformations have occurred in American business over the past two decades. Changes that have impacted business careers include:

- the shift from a manufacturing to a service economy
- the globalization of business
- the restructuring of corporations

- the acceleration of high technology
- the diversification in the work force
- the variations in life-styles of American families

These transformations affect the types of products offered, the nature of jobs involved in producing and marketing them, the demand for individuals with certain skills, the salaries offered workers—even the size and location of businesses themselves. Throughout this book, trends affecting specific fields are highlighted, salaries and mand statistics cited, and opportunities for individuals in certain areas discussed.

CAREER MOBILITY

Quoting the well-known management specialist Peter Drucker, "The probability that the first job choice you make is right for you is roughly one in a million. If you decide your first choice is the right one, chances are you are just plain lazy."[2] Movement from one job to another—upward, downward, or laterally—or movement from one field to another are ways in which a career develops. Upward mobility has always been regarded as desirable or indicative of success. This has not always been the case with other types of movement.

Today mobility of all types is likely to be considered indicative of personal development rather than instability, as it was in the past. Still, mobility in itself is neither good nor bad—it depends on the individual's circumstances. Ambition, quality of life or lifestyle considerations, and desire for new challenges all may affect the career path that an individual chooses to follow.

One factor that will greatly influence mobility in business careers in the future is the restructuring of American corporations, which began in the 1980s and will continue throughout the 1990s. Acquisitions and buyouts changed many corporate identities. Recession and competition from abroad forced downsizing and restructuring. Hundreds of thousands of managers and professionals were forced to change jobs or to retire early. Vacancies throughout management levels were not refilled. While 12 to 15 levels of supervision were typical in large corporations in the 1970s, today 5 or 6 levels are more common.

The reduction in numbers of midlevel managers will make advancement in the corporate hierarchy increasingly more competitive. Most college graduates will remain in the same jobs for longer periods of time, perhaps five years instead of the two years spent in the same position by the upwardly mobile workers of the 1970s. Also, fewer types of positions will be available to new graduates. The upside of this issue is that even entry-level jobs will be more varied and challenging. Managers with too

[2]Mary Harrington Hall, "A Conversation with Peter Drucker," *Psychology Today*, March 1968, p. 22.

much to do will be forced to delegate many tasks to lower-level and beginning employees. Project teams will be used more widely as companies attempt a more entrepreneurial approach to product development. Work will be less structured. More freedom, as a result of reduced numbers of supervisors, will enable employees to show better what they are able to do.

Each chapter of this book describing specific career areas contains information regarding career mobility. This information enables individuals to use the career decision-making model in a forward-looking way. Instead of merely opting for an entry-level position, you can focus on a possible career path.

Though the book suggests many ways to advance to positions higher up in the company, there are many individuals who find satisfying jobs in business and are content to remain in the same position throughout their careers. This is often the case with highly specialized or technical jobs. Many people who earn associate degrees from community colleges enter such positions. The important thing is that an individual be satisfied with what he or she is doing. Career development and growth can occur as an individual becomes more proficient in a specific job.

The choice of whether or not to vie for management positions depends on the values, educational background, and abilities of the individual. Advancement from one position to another often can depend on a willingness to gain additional education. An individual may choose to work toward an advanced degree to increase the chance of entering the management ranks. Sometimes the company will pay for this additional education. Because more and more people are earning a bachelor's degree in business, employers are beginning to hire only people with business degrees for many of the positions described in this book. Some positions also require graduate degrees. There are, however, still some positions in business for people with only an associate degree, as you will see in the following chapters. High school graduates with no further education are unlikely to go far in today's business world.

BUSINESS CAREERS IN TODAY'S ECONOMY

Many economic factors impact business careers. We live in a service-oriented economy. Roughly 75 percent of all jobs in our economy are in a service industry. It is likely that this percentage will rise even higher in the future. New college graduates in the 1990s will find opportunities in such fields as health care services, convention planning, financial services, and others that they may never have considered or know very little about. To better understand opportunities in the service sector, it is necessary to differentiate between a good and a service. A good is a physical product. A service is an activity performed for an individual or firm. While a physical product is impersonal, a service is usually personal. Service industries may be equipment-based, people-based, or a combination of both. For example, electronic data bases, automated bank tellers, and diagnostic medical equipment are the tools of equipment-based service industries. An advertising agency is people-based.

Services are intangible. Banks and airlines cannot give samples or claim physical qualities that outlast those of the competition. Services cannot be repossessed if bills are unpaid. Although services cannot be stored as inventory, they must be produced on demand. Long lines or an inability to accommodate customers can seriously impair a service business. Services cannot be mailed; they must be delivered on the spot at a convenient location. Quality is very hard to control—similar services can vary greatly from organization to organization, employee to employee, and even for the same employee.

Most new college graduates will be employed in service industries. The demand for services sales representatives is predicted to grow much faster than average. It is important to identify an industry as well as a field and prepare yourself for its unique demands. Areas where demand will be particularly strong for sales representatives are temporary help services, business and financial services, information services, and advertising sales. Hotel and automotive service sales also will grow at a faster-than-average rate. Technology-based service companies, and indeed companies in all industries, will be affected by advances in information and communications technology.

Advances in information and communications technology have revolutionized the workplace of today and created opportunities for companies and individuals that simply did not exist a mere decade ago. Computers are faster, cheaper, smaller, and infinitely more versatile than ever before. They impact virtually every aspect of business today. Managers have immediate access to information that enables them to make better business decisions. Vast communications networks connect every aspect of company operations and enable head offices and branches all over the world to remain in close contact. Business majors who are not able to use these new technologies to perform better in a business environment will miss many career opportunities.

Not only has the American economy become both service- and technology-oriented, it has in recent years become globally oriented as well. Competition from European and Asian markets has caused U.S. companies to expand their operations abroad, start new ones, or enter foreign markets through acquisitions and mergers instead of merely exporting their products. The 1992 integration of the European Community will remove trade barriers from country to country in Europe.

Many U.S.-based companies are already multinational—that is, have operations in other countries—including Ford Motor Company, Merck & Company, Coca-Cola, IBM, and Hewlett-Packard, who have had successful operations in Europe for years. In Japan, McDonald's, Disney, Dupont, and Amway have prospered. According to a 1990 survey conducted by *The Wall Street Journal*, one-third of corporate chief executive officers (CEOs) plan to build or buy factories in Eastern Europe over the next five years. Closer to home, recent progress toward free trade agreements with Mexico, similar to those between the United States and Canada, could wipe out such trade barriers as protective tariffs and create a unified North American economy. These changes are likely to alter the nature of the global marketplace and create many new opportunities at home and abroad for business graduates.

Although in the recent past there has been an oversupply of college graduates, the supply has leveled off and projections suggest that it will shrink over the next 10 years. Overall, the demand for business and management majors has been consistently strong. Demand for 1991 business and management graduates is estimated at 24 percent of total demand for graduates. Enrollments in colleges of business across the country indicate that there will be ample graduates to fill this demand. However, other figures suggest that supply will not keep pace with demand in many areas, particularly the demand for entry-level workers. As demand grows, a percentage decline will continue in the young adult population between the ages of 16 and 24, from 30 percent of the labor force in 1985 to 16 percent in the year 2000. In general, more choices and higher salaries usually accompany supply shortages.

PERSONAL FACTORS TO CONSIDER IN CAREER PLANNING

In addition to the economic factors, personal factors should play an important part in career planning. Life-style preferences and personal attributes affect career success and happiness. Individual life-styles and values have been changing over the years. More and more people are viewing work as a way to maintain a particular life-style rather than developing life-styles consistent with work. The role of fathers has changed as mothers have entered the work force. In families with two-career couples, both partners share in family responsibilities. Though studies show that it is still the mother who misses work most frequently when children are ill, fathers definitely are doing more shopping. Statistics also show that the divorce rate is lessening. All these changes affect how people plan their careers and balance work and family responsibilities.

Opportunities in business careers exist virtually everywhere in companies of all sizes. However, considerable trade-offs in terms of quality of life, cost of living, and the merits of the job must all be considered. Salaries tend to be highest where the cost of living is greatest, as expected. The location of a job either adds to or detracts from its desirability, depending on personal values and priorities. Overall, some of the best employment opportunities will be in Los Angeles, Washington D.C., Seattle, Houston, and Detroit, according to an article in *Managing Your Career*, the Spring 1990 college edition of the *National Business Employment Weekly* published by *The Wall Street Journal*.

Professionals with working spouses and children are more likely to refuse promotions that require moving to another or less desirable city. Many professionals start their own businesses for both personal and professional reasons. Women with children often work or run their own businesses at home. Working at home is possible for many people through information and communications technology. Today more than ever before, career decisions are likely to weigh both personal and professional factors.

THE ROLE OF SELF-EVALUATION IN CAREER CHOICE

The development of a satisfying career greatly affects an individual's feeling of self-worth and the attainment of a desired life-style. Successful career development depends in part on an individual's ability for accurate self-evaluation. Self-evaluation is, for the most part, a do-it-yourself project. Although you may seek the help of friends, family, and professional counselors, you are the ultimate authority on yourself. Self-concept develops in an interesting way. An individual is mirrored to an extent by others—that is, the messages from others reflecting their perception of that individual in part contribute to the development of an individual's self-concept. But it is the translation of these messages by the individual that plays the most significant role in the development of self-concept.

A person's self-concept is very much involved in career choice. It is affected by past successes and failures. We tend to build upon past successes in developing our careers. These successes are related to our abilities, values, and personality characteristics. We can improve our abilities, or change our values, but our personalities—though this is a topic of much debate—are set from an early age according to Drucker.

> . . . I am convinced that one can acquire knowledge, one can acquire skills, but one cannot change his personality. . . . I have had four great children, and I can assure you that by the time they were six months old, they were set in concrete. . . . [3]

Whether or not you agree with Drucker, it would be wise to carefully consider yourself—those things you can change or want to change and those things you can't change or don't want to change, and let these things help determine your career choice. In fact, success or failure in a career often depends on how well an individual is able to self-evaluate.

The purpose of this section is not psychoanalytic, but practical, because you must be realistic about yourself in order to use the following career decision-making model in the most meaningful way.

---

[3]Ibid., p. 23.

Figure 1-2 Career decision-making model

Internal factors	External factors
Aptitudes and attributes _____ Academic aptitudes and achievement _____ Occupational aptitudes and skills _____ Social skills _____ Communication skills _____ Leadership abilities _____ _____ _____ _____ _____ _____ _____ _____	**Family influence** _____ Family values and expectations _____ Socioeconomic level _____ _____ _____ _____ _____ _____ _____ _____ _____ _____ _____ _____
Interests _____ Amount of supervision _____ Amount of pressure _____ Amount of variety _____ Amount of work with data _____ Amount of work with people _____ _____ _____ _____ _____ _____	**Economic influence** _____ Overall economic conditions _____ Employment trends _____ Job market information _____ _____ _____ _____ _____ _____ _____ _____

Values
 	
_____ Salary
_____ Status/prestige
_____ Advancement opportunity
_____ Growth on the job
_____ _____
_____ _____
_____ _____
_____ _____
	Societal influence
	
	_____ Perceived effect of race, sex, or
	        ethnic background on success
	_____ Perceived effect of physical or
	        psychological disabilities on success
	_____ _____
	_____ _____
	_____ _____
	_____ _____

AN OPEN MODEL FOR CAREER DECISION MAKING

So many factors determine career decisions that the only sensible, systematic approach for making these complex decisions is through a model that incorporates factors significant in a personal sense to the decision maker. The career-decision-making model shown in Figure 1-2 includes the most common factors considered in career decisions. It is "open" in that it provides space for you to add significant factors that you feel might have been omitted, thus adapting the model to yourself.

The model is divided into internal factors and external factors. The internal factors include those things about your personal makeup that will have an impact on your career choice. The external factors include those outside forces—family, economy, and society—that impact career decisions.

Internal Factors

The first category is *Aptitudes and attributes*. Items in this category reveal answers to the question, "What am I able to do, given the talents and characteristics I have?" The talents and characteristics you possess will be more consistent with demands for success in some jobs than in others.

The second category is *Interests*. Items in this category suggest the question, "What would I like to do on the job?" Does pressure stimulate you intellectually or cause you anxiety? Would you prefer to work in a variety of areas (generalist), or would you rather be an expert in one area (specialist)? Do you prefer greater structure on the job or more freedom?

The final category is *Values*. These items suggest the question, "What do I need for job satisfaction?" Values vary greatly from individual to individual. This is one area in particular that you might want to add some of your own factors to the model in the space provided.

External Factors

The first category, *Family influence*, refers to expectations that your family might have of you or that you might have of yourself, instilled by your ethnic background, the socioeconomic level at which you grew up, or the occupations of your parents.

The second category is *Economic influence*, an area that is constantly changing and one that you should carefully consider in making any career decisions. What do overall economic conditions tell you about your future in a certain industry? How consistent is your background with trends in employment? What effect will advancing technology have on your ability to advance in your job or in the industry in which you are employed? Is the job market an employer's or a job seeker's market in your area? What are the chances of employment in your chosen field after graduation?

The final external factor is *Societal influence*. How successful are women and minorities in your chosen field? Will your sex, race, or ethnic background help or hinder you in getting the job you want and advancing in it? To what extent will impaired hearing or vision or any other disability limit you in the career area of your choice?

Adapting the Model to Yourself

To prepare this model for use in evaluating the career options described throughout this book, you must do the following:

1. Add any factors that you feel are relevant to your individual career decision-making process and have not already been included in this model in the spaces provided.
2. Weigh each factor, including the ones that you added to the model, by entering a weight of from 0 to 5 in the space to the left of the factor according to the following scale:

    0 = Totally unimportant to career decisions
    1 = Slightly important to career decisions
    2 = Somewhat important to career decisions
    3 = Moderately important to career decisions
    4 = Substantially important to career decisions
    5 = Extremely important to career decisions

To help you weigh the factors, let's consider each factor one at a time. Add any factors that you wish to your model as we discuss each area. Beginning with the internal factors, under *Aptitudes and attributes*, consider the explanations and assign a weight to each factor as we go along.

Academic aptitudes and achievement. This refers to how well you have done or can do in school and where your weak and strong areas are. To what extent do you feel that your academic aptitudes and achievement will affect your choice of a career?

Occupational aptitudes and skills. This refers to how well you can perform or can learn to perform certain job-related tasks. How important do you feel that your occupational aptitudes and skills are in your choice of a career?

Social skills. This refers to how well you are able to get along with people—your human relations skills. To what extent do you feel that your social skills will affect your career choice?

Communication skills. This refers to how well you are able to communicate with others through speaking, writing, and body language. How important do you feel communication skills are in choosing your career?

Leadership abilities. This refers to how well you are able to influence others to think or act in a certain way or to follow your lead. To what extent do you feel your leadership abilities will affect your choice of a career?

Other. Assign a weight to any factors that you have added to your model in the space provided under *Aptitudes and attributes*.

Under *Interests*, consider the following explanations and weigh the factors as we go along.

Amount of supervision.   This refers to the extent to which you take orders from someone else or work on your own. If you have no preference one way or the other, assign a weight of 0 to the factor. If you prefer more or less supervision, assign a weight from 1 to 5, depending on how important the amount of supervision is to your career choice.

Amount of pressure.   This refers to the pressure that is part of most jobs to some extent. However, some jobs are low-pressure, some are high-pressure. Weigh this factor according to how important the amount of pressure on the job might be to your career choice.

Amount of variety.   Some jobs have many varied duties, some have only a few specific duties. Some jobs have duties that change periodically, while others are fairly routine. To what extent will the amount of variety affect your career choice?

Amount of work with data.   Although all careers in business require working with raw data or with data that have been processed into information, some business careers are based primarily on working with data rather than with people. To what extent will the amount of work with data affect your career choice?

Amount of work with people.   Although all careers in business require working with people to some extent, some careers involve primarily working with people. How important is the amount of work with people in choosing your career?

Other.   Assign a weight to any factors that you have added to your model in the spaces provided under *Interests*.

Under *Values*, consider the following explanations and weight the factors as we go along.

Salary.   How important is the salary you will receive to your career choice?

Status/prestige.   Status or prestige suggests the need to feel important among colleagues. To what extent will this factor affect your career choice?

Advancement opportunity.   Some careers afford much opportunity for advancement; others provide little. How important is advancement opportunity in your career choice?

Growth on the job.   Many career areas offer training, education, and special opportunities for growth or professional development. To what extent is this important in selecting your career?

Other.   Assign a weight to any factors that you have added to your model in the spaces provided under *Values*. You definitely should have added a few factors to your model.

Now let's consider the external factors. Under *Family influence*, consider the explanations and weigh the factors as we go along.

Family values and expectations.   Consider the expectations that your family has of you. The values that they possess define these expectations. Are you expected to follow in your father's or mother's footsteps or to enter the family business? Do you currently have or anticipate a family of your own? Are you a partner in a dual-career-couple relationship? To what extent do the values and expectations of your family play a part in your choice of a career?

Socioeconomic level.   You have grown up in a certain economic level of society. This level was established to some extent by your parents' occupations and income. Do you want to continue living in the style to which you have grown accustomed, or would you like to become accustomed to a more affluent style of living? To what extent does the socioeconomic level of your family affect your career choice?

Other.   Assign a weight to any factors that you have added to your model in the spaces provided under *Family influence*.

Under *Economic influence*, consider the explanations and weigh the factors as we go along.

Overall economic conditions.   Overall economic conditions affect some careers more than others. For example, retail sales tend to drop during economic downturns. To what extent do you feel that overall economic conditions will affect your choice of a career?

Employment trends.   Many trends have an impact on patterns of employment. Changing technology often changes the nature of careers. As some knowledge becomes obsolete and other knowledge is in demand, the preparation for some careers changes. Some careers vanish and others appear. To what extent do you feel this knowledge of employment trends is important in selecting your career?

Job market information.   The job opportunities that are available now and in the future can be found in a number of sources, such as the *Occupational Outlook Handbook* published by the U.S. government. This job market information gives an indication of the number of annual openings expected in various career areas and the competition for these openings. How important is this job market information to your choice of a career?

Other. Assign a weight to any factors that you have added in the spaces provided under *Economic influence*.

Under *Societal influence*, consider the following explanations and weigh the factors as we go along.

Perceived effect of race, sex, or ethnic background on success. This factor refers to what effect you feel your race, sex, or ethnic background will have on your success in certain career areas in business. How important is this factor in your choice of a career?

Perceived effect of physical or psychological disabilities on success. There are some careers that would be difficult to handle for those with certain kinds of disabilities. If you possess a physical disability—such as loss of a limb or impaired vision or hearing—or a psychological disability—such as a tendency to break down under stress—you would want to include this factor in your career decision-making model. The degree to which the disability might affect success will probably differ from one career to the next. If you have no physical or psychological disabilities, assign a weight of 0 to this factor.

Other. Assign a weight to any factors that you might have added in the spaces provided under *Societal influence*.

No One Said This Was Going to Be Easy

This model may seem complicated to you, but so is choosing a career. As you read the material in each chapter and use the career decision-making model to evaluate the particular career area described, you also will have to use a good bit of judgment. You may have to do some additional research to complete the evaluation, particularly if you have added some factors that might not be addressed in the chapter. For the most part, the information in the following chapters will enable you to use the model effectively.

Note that getting career decision making down to a science of numbers does not reduce the amount of time you should spend in thoughtful consideration of the way you weigh the factors, the information you acquire from this book, and your own self-evaluation.

Optional Activities

If you encountered any difficulties weighing factors in the model, you might find some of the following activities helpful:

Activity A. Write 10 statements that begin, "I am...."

Activity B. List 10 things that you would like to do before you die.

Activity C.   List 10 conditions that mean the most to you in your work.

These simple activities are designed to assist you in self-evaluation. Through them, you might define some priorities in your life, which would suggest factors that should be added to your decision-making model.

GETTING DOWN TO BUSINESS

Exploring careers in business is fascinating because of the variety of possibilities. Beginning with the interest in business that you already have demonstrated (you found this book!), you will be increasingly surprised, even bewildered, by the myriad of choices available to you. Each of the following nine chapters will explore a field in business. It will describe various positions in the field, career paths, salaries, trends, job opportunities, aptitudes and attributes needed for success, and sources of additional information. At the end of the chapter, you will evaluate the career area using your weighted career decision-making model.

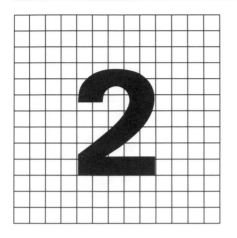

CAREERS IN ACCOUNTING

CHAPTER OBJECTIVES

Upon completion of this chapter, you should be able to:

1. Describe the work of accountants.
2. Discuss trends in accounting and their impact on the career in general.
3. Diagram career paths for accountants in government, public accounting firms, and private industry.
4. Discuss job opportunities within the accounting field today.
5. List the educational preparation and skills needed to enter the field of accounting.
6. Evaluate careers in accounting according to your individualized career decision-making model.

Gone forever are the green eyeshades and thick glasses, and with them the image of the accountant as an introverted mathematician, surrounded by reams of paper, whose contact and communication with the outside world are minimal. Accounting is regarded by some as the dynamic career of the decade. Over 1.3 million auditors and accountants are employed nationwide, according to recent Bureau of Labor statistics, and the number is projected to increase by 40 percent between 1986 and the year 2000. The accountant's new role in the complex and changing world of today is envisioned by those seeking to enter the accounting ranks as one of change agent, communications expert, systems professional, management consultant, government conscience—at best, glamorous and prestigious, and, at the very least, secure and lucrative.

This chapter will enable you to look closely at accounting as a prospective career. It includes such information as

- what services accountants provide
- who employs them
- salaries and career paths
- latest trends
- job opportunities
- education and skills needed to pursue a career in accounting
- sources of additional information on accounting careers

THE JOB

An accountant may provide many services throughout the course of a career but can hardly be expected to be an expert in all. As an accountant's career progresses, there is a tendency to specialize in one area. Some areas in which accountants work are discussed in the sections below.

Auditing	Auditors test the accuracy of accounts and determine whether established procedures and systems were followed. They may detect waste and fraud. An auditor is responsible for checking the accounts periodically and for giving a professional opinion as to whether they accurately reflect the company's financial position. Audits may be conducted by internal auditing personnel or by external auditors, that is, certified public accountants (CPAs) from public accounting firms who report their findings to top-level company executives and outside groups such as the Internal Revenue Service (IRS) and the Securities and Exchange Commission (SEC). Audits are required by the SEC for all companies offering their stock for sale to the public.
Tax Accounting	Tax accountants prepare tax returns, research tax problems to identify maximum tax advantages, and confer with Internal Revenue Service examiners on behalf of employers and individuals. Most CPAs in public accounting firms are involved in tax accounting. Tax accountants must keep current, since the tax laws change annually, and help clients make wise and timely decisions with respect to these changes. Estate and corporate planning to minimize or delay taxes is an important part of this job.
Systems and Procedures Accounting	The responsibility of a systems and procedures accountant is to design and install accounting systems, usually computerized, that enable the firm to keep good financial records. As the business grows or the laws change, systems and procedures accountants review and expand the accounting systems and procedures. They are involved in the purchase, installation, and use of computers and information systems.
Cost Accounting	Cost accountants work primarily with production records and inventory accounts. They are responsible for measuring, allocating, and assigning production and overhead costs to units of inventory to enable management to make decisions concerning whether new products should be produced or existing products should continue to be produced and for how much they should be sold. Cost-benefit analyses are frequently conducted in business to get to the proverbial bottom line—or bottom two lines, joked an accountant, in reference to the two lines typically found at the bottom of pages used by accountants for such analyses.
Budget and Forecast Accounting	A budget and forecast accountant plans for the future, prepares both short-term and long-term budgets, provides for the organization's cash requirements, projects market forecasts, and accumulates a variety of other analytical information needed by management to make sound fi-

nancial decisions. Budget and forecast accountants are widely employed in both private and government sectors.

General Accounting

General accountants perform some or all of the activities described for other specialties, including keeping records on a daily basis, developing and supervising accounting practices, and preparing financial statements and special reports such as balance sheets and income statements, profit and loss statements, cash flow statements, cost-benefit analyses, and others.

Managerial Accounting

A managerial accountant provides operational advice to management on a variety of matters over the range of an organization's complete operation and is considered a member of the management team. The top accounting position in an organization is the *controller*. The controller directs the total accounting program, including all of the activities described previously. Computer-oriented management consulting is offered through the consulting divisions of major accounting firms. Many managerial accountants find positions with such firms.

Public Accounting

Certified public accountants (CPAs) are employed by public accounting firms or work in independent practice. CPAs perform one or all of the services described for other specialities for clients or employers, usually on a repeat basis. Much of the work performed by certified public accountants is auditing and tax accounting. Today, large public accounting firms are offering more services to more types of organizations than ever before. Specialization by industry or accounting function is common. For diversity of experience, public accounting offers the most opportunity since CPAs work with a variety of people and companies. Pressure, travel, and seven-day workweeks often go with the job.

CAREER PATHS AND COMPENSATION

Today approximately 20 percent of practicing accountants are employed by public accounting firms; approximately 65 percent by profit-seeking and not-for-profit organizations; most of the rest by local, state, and federal governments; and a small number by colleges and universities offering educational programs in accounting (Chapter 10 discusses college teaching as a career). Because the same functions are performed by accountants employed by public accounting firms, organizations, and government, there is considerable lateral mobility as well as upward mobility for accountants with the training, talent, and drive to strive for the highest positions. Figure 2-1 indicates the various positions in which you might be employed as an accountant, salary ranges for those posi-

Figure 2-1   Accounting positions, salaries, and mobility

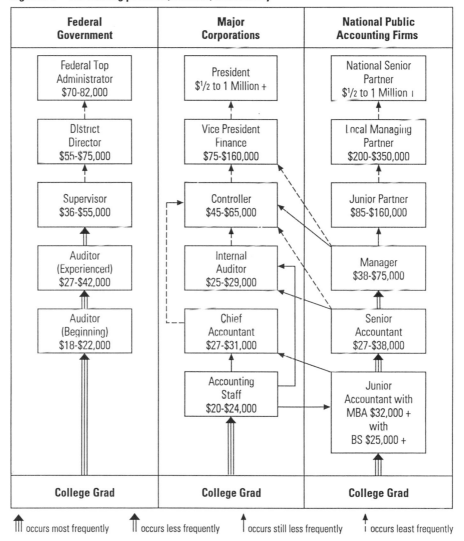

Federal Government	Major Corporations	National Public Accounting Firms
Federal Top Administrator $70-82,000	President $1/2 to 1 Million +	National Senior Partner $1/2 to 1 Million
District Director $55-$75,000	Vice President Finance $75-$160,000	Local Managing Partner $200-$350,000
Supervisor $36-$55,000	Controller $45-$65,000	Junior Partner $85-$160,000
Auditor (Experienced) $27-$42,000	Internal Auditor $25-$29,000	Manager $38-$75,000
Auditor (Beginning) $18-$22,000	Chief Accountant $27-$31,000	Senior Accountant $27-$38,000
	Accounting Staff $20-$24,000	Junior Accountant with MBA $32,000 + with BS $25,000 +
College Grad	College Grad	College Grad

⫼ occurs most frequently   ‖ occurs less frequently | occurs still less frequently   ¦ occurs least frequently

tions, and patterns of mobility. Note that the different types of arrows reflect the frequency of occurrence of the upward and lateral mobility.

Clearly, there is room for only a few at the top. However, many top executives began in accounting. William Lavin, chief financial officer for Woolworth Corp., one of the world's retailing giants, began his career in public accounting, where he gained a well-rounded education for business before moving to finance. A 1990 *Business Week* survey of chief executive officers (CEOs) at the 1,000 most valuable U.S. companies showed that 31 percent were promoted through the finance-accounting ranks.

Typically, but not always, accountants who work for the federal government, major corporations, and multinational public accounting firms earn higher salaries than do accountants in local public accounting firms, small companies, and state and local governments. In recent years, accounting salaries in general have been characterized by moderate annual increases. An average starting salary for new bachelor's degree graduates is $28,133. This figure was estimated using data from *Recruiting Trends 1989-90*, compiled by Michigan State University.

Mobility and salary are only two factors to consider in comparing job offers, however. Government work, though lower in salary, offers numerous fringe benefits and is usually more stable. Likewise, though accountants in private practice may not always earn as much as those employed by large companies, they have a great deal of freedom. Recent figures show that salaries for public accountants have eroded over 10 percent during the past decade, compared with salaries in the financial service industry, which are ever on the rise. More graduates also are being attracted by the shorter hours, faster advancement, and exciting new opportunities in private industry. In response, some accounting firms have increased entry-level salaries and vacation time and replaced overtime pay with bonuses based on performance.

The Big Six

The largest and most prestigious multinational public accounting firms were known for years as the Big Eight. Through mergers to gear up for increased global competition, they recently have become the Big Six. Listed by size from largest to smallest, they include:

1. Ernst & Young
2. Arthur Andersen & Co.
3. Coopers & Lybrand
4. KPMG Peat Marwick
5. Deloitte & Touche
6. Price Waterhouse & Co.

The big firms get the top 10 percent of all accounting graduates. Tough competition eliminates 50 percent of the new recruits within three years. Why are these beginners willing to face these types of pressure and odds? The large firms invest millions of dollars in training, giving junior accountants invaluable education and experience in sophisticated accounting techniques. Even if you are one of the 50 percent who leave the large companies within the first three years, you take away with you and into your next job this education and experience. The 95 percent who never make partner in Big Six firms eventually become partners in smaller firms, go into independent practice, join private industry financial staffs, or enter government jobs.

There is a great deal of prestige attached to working with a big public accounting firm or working at an executive level in an organization. There is also a great deal of pressure. Recall that accountants do very well in private industry in moving up the corporate ladder. About 50 percent of those who leave a big public accounting firm end up on the staff of one of the firm's clients, so they begin in many cases with the advantage of knowing the accounting system and a good bit about their new employer.

One strategy of recent college graduates is to try to find a job with one of the large public accounting firms for the education and experience, then go into private practice or to work in corporate America. Keep in mind, though, that many major corporations and government agencies have strict promotion-from-within policies and normally will not hire someone from a public accounting firm for an advanced position, but rather will promote an accountant already working in the company. In such companies, everyone starts at entry level, so if you have a company in mind that you would like to work for, it would be a good idea to check out the company's promotion policy. Evaluating job offers and companies will be discussed in Chapter 12.

CURRENT TRENDS

The role of the accountant is changing in a number of ways. With the increasing U.S. national debt and the overwhelming task of streamlining federal government spending, today's CPA is expected to go beyond the financial audit and to tackle measuring the efficiency, economy, and effectiveness of government programs. According to Thomas W. Rimerman, the chair of the American Institute of Certified Public Accountants (AICPA), the organization will continue to serve as a catalyst for federal financial management reform. CPAs recently have been placed in the forefront of this national issue. Accountants must learn new standards and techniques of measurement. While computers have reduced some of the routine tasks, greater communication with employees in the programs will be required.

The managerial accountant's new role as a full member of the management team also increases the need for communication skills. Furthermore, the involvement of the accountant in organizational change includes planning and controlling, designing information systems, and suggesting responsibility accounting centers for performance evaluation. As the job becomes more complicated, the tendency to specialize becomes greater. The Certified Management Accountant (CMA) certificate is becoming more widespread as the field gains more professional status.

There is a trend both in industry and in public accounting toward specialization. In industry, such specialists as tax accountants, systems and forecast accountants, and internal auditors complement the activities of cost and managerial accountants. In public accounting, specialist areas outside the main function of general auditing include tax accounting, management consulting, systems development, marketing, and research and training. There is also a tendency in public accounting to specialize by industry.

The technological and information revolution has brought about the need for changes in financial statement models. Today's accountants are dealing with volatile prices, currency fluctuations, and changing property values—all of which can be transmitted instantaneously at the computer keyboard and have immediate impact on financial markets. In addition, more complex financial transactions and instruments are changing the requirements for meaningful financial reports. Opportunities will abound for accountants who have the ability to use the new information technologies to utmost advantage.

The advantages of specialization are high initial salaries and great demand for services. An accountant can spend two or three years in a specialist field without restricting opportunities to get back into the mainstream of auditing or financial management. However, a longer time as a specialist might restrict these opportunities by limiting the range of the accountant's experience too much. If you want to specialize, it is important that you identify both the short-term and the long-term roles that you want to play in the field of accounting. The trends described in this section have affected accounting education and the skills that you will need if you choose accounting as a career.

JOB OPPORTUNITIES

According to statistics cited in the 1990 *Occupational Outlook Handbook*, there were 963,000 auditors and accountants in 1988. Most accountants work in urban areas. Roughly 10 percent are self-employed and fewer than 10 percent work part time. States licensed over 300,000 CPAs and more than 20,000 public accountants or registered public accountants, the latter mostly managerial and government accountants. Though the registered public accountant designation is currently recognized in 38 states, it is being phased out. Other designations in accounting are not state-regulated, but granted by professional societies. Approximate numbers of accountants holding such designations include:

> 15,000 Certified Internal Auditors
> 8,000 Certified Management Accountants
> 5,000 Certified Information Systems Auditors
> 4,000 Certificates of Accreditation in accounting or taxation awarded by the Accreditation Council for Accountancy

Efforts are currently underway by accounting professionals to institute a Uniform Accountancy Act that stipulates licensing requirements in the 54 separate jurisdictions of the United States.

Demand

Much of the demand for accounting services is created by the passage of new laws and regulations. For example, tax laws change so frequently and are so complex that every year fewer and fewer Americans even attempt to do their own tax returns. As many as 100 tax accountants can work for a single large firm. Also, every year additional requirements by the Securities and Exchange Commission for recordkeeping and disclosure practices in corporations that sell their stock to the public cause the demand for CPAs to increase. New auditing requirements for pension plans and for public campaign fund records further increase the need for CPAs. When Jimmy Carter was president in the 1970s, his campaign CPA jokingly referred to the 1974 Campaign Reform Act as the "Lawyers' and CPAs' Full Employment Bill." The 1986 Tax Reform Act, which purported to simplify the tax laws, and the continued subsequent changes have confused both individuals and companies, thus increasing the need for accountants.

Aside from increased demand for accountants due to laws and regulations, public pressure is building to force public companies to issue audited quarterly financial statements. Pressure from Wall Street, banks, and politicians is building to force local and state governments that want to borrow money in public markets to issue certified financial statements.

Numerous new financial instruments have created the need for money managers who may have backgrounds in either accounting or finance. Information technology and what it has to offer have motivated many accounting firms to create management information systems departments that offer consulting services to assist companies in the design and implementation of accounting information systems.

Supply

With continued faster-than-average growth in demand, today's graduates are insufficient in numbers to fill the available positions. Rick Elam speculated on the future supply of CPAs in an article entitled, "Will There Be a Shortage of CPAs?" appearing in the August 1990 issue of the *Journal of Accountancy*. The number of accounting graduates has declined over the past several years. However, a 1989 survey conducted by the American Council of Education (ACE) showed that accounting ranked second out of 80 probable majors chosen by 6.1 percent of the freshmen surveyed. Business, the number one choice, was selected by 6.5 percent. The new 150-hour education requirement did not seem to deter the students. In fact, the ACE study showed that 60 percent of the freshmen surveyed intended to obtain graduate degrees. Of course, many of these freshmen will not end up with accounting degrees.

The total number of accounting degrees awarded is expected to remain constant at about 45,000 annually. Though it is estimated that by the year 2000 the number of candidates sitting for the CPA exam will be considerably fewer than the current 145,000 annual takers, increased degree requirements and improved accounting programs will increase the number who actually pass the exam and become licensed CPAs. On this assumption, it has been projected that there will be enough new CPAs during the next 20 years to supply the needs of the profession.

Beware of the job market, as it is a constantly fluctuating thing. Often when demand in a particular area is great, more students major in that area to be assured of a good job after graduation. A pendulum effect occurs. When too many job seekers flock to a hot demand area, the market becomes glutted, the pendulum swings to the other extreme, and demand falls to a low point. This has happened in the past in such fields as engineering. There is then a cooling-off period, fewer students enter academic programs, and fewer new applicants enter the field over a period of years. This causes demand to increase and the pendulum swings again.

Given the current supply-and-demand situation, accountants are hardly being pressured into early retirement. On the contrary, retired accounting executives are being recruited by the International Executive Service Corps to serve as consultants in foreign companies.

Equal Opportunity Standing

If you are a woman or member of a minority group, you are likely to be actively recruited for an accounting position. In 1987, roughly 45.7 percent of accountants were women and 7.4 percent were African Americans. Women have done well generally in the accounting profession. Involved in professional organizations, women have begun two societies for women accountants, the American Society of Women Accountants and the American Woman's Society of Certified Public Accountants. Further evidence of the high degree of professionalism among women accountants is the high percentage of women involved in continuing education programs and in such professional activities as writing articles and giving speeches. If you are female, you will be happy to hear that past surveys indicate that a larger percentage of women than men pass the CPA exam the first time around. If you are male, know that you are in for some competition from women. Women in greater numbers are moving into management in organizations and being promoted to partner in large accounting firms.

Studies have shown that African Americans are being hired by national CPA firms but tend not to be hired as much by local firms. It has been speculated that they have not been hired to a greater extent in public accounting in general because of a failure on the part of the companies in the past to actively recruit at colleges with an African American majority. A recent study shows that the percentage of African American accountants has risen from 0.15 percent in 1968 to 0.6 percent today, a modest gain considering other professions such as law (2 percent) and medicine (3.3 percent). Reasons why larger numbers of African Americans have not entered the accounting profession include racial bias, lack of mobility of African American accountants, lack of strong affirmative action programs, and lack of an awareness of career opportunities by African American youth. In addition, accounting firms run by African Americans have not experienced much growth over the past few years compared with accounting firms as a whole.

What does all this mean to you? If you opt for a career in accounting today, there is a strong likelihood that a job in accounting will be waiting for you when you complete your college program. Another factor that might keep the market from being glutted is the casualty rate among would-be accounting majors. Many students lack the analytical abilities and the persistence for accuracy with numbers required for success in an accounting program, thus the casualty rate is sizable. Don't become a casualty statistic! Be sure you have the necessary aptitudes and characteristics for success before choosing accounting as your major.

APTITUDES AND ATTRIBUTES NEEDED FOR SUCCESS

Education

To prepare for a career in accounting, you must complete a college program with a major in accounting and obtain a bachelor of arts (BA) or bachelor of science (BS) degree. Many professional accounting programs, which are five-year programs, are being developed throughout the country. These longer programs came about for the following reasons:

- the expansion of knowledge required in accounting today
- the complex interrelationships between business, government, and society
- the increased need for communication skills
- the need to better prepare students for the CPA examination

An MBA (master of business administration) with an accounting undergraduate degree or a master of accounting degree can increase your chances of being hired, particularly by a big public accounting firm. Although traditional four-year accounting programs are still prevalent in the educational scene, many accounting professors feel that people who ultimately become partners in large accounting firms or rise to leadership positions in government and industry in the future will have completed a master's degree or professional accounting program.

A college program   should include a core of liberal arts courses, with emphasis on written and oral communications, and at least the following accounting and finance courses:

- the two beginning accounting courses
- an intermediate course
- cost accounting
- courses in auditing and tax

- a beginning course in the principles of finance
- computer science or information systems electives

Liberal arts graduates with courses in economics, calculus, statistics, and computer science may be recruited by large public accounting firms and put through a demanding training program. Some universities offer highly competitive 12- to 15-month accounting programs. Acceptance into such a program is often contingent on an employment offer from a public accounting firm.

Internships   in accounting are available with accounting firms, corporations, and government agencies. These internships may be found through college and university placement offices, professors, state CPA societies, or direct contact with companies. Large public accounting firms and the U.S. General Accounting Office select college juniors and seniors for internship programs.

Extracurricular activities.   Although your grade point average is important, other qualifications are equally important. Many interviewers, particularly from public accounting firms, regard extracurricular involvement in student organizations in a very favorable light. If you hold office in a student organization, this indicates that you work well with others and are able to gain their confidence and respect. These qualities are essential for success in public accounting since you must be able to sell your professional accounting ability to clients.

Skills and attributes   necessary for success in a college accounting program as well as success in an accounting position after graduation include:

- analytical ability
- communication ability
- organizational ability
- ability to "think in numbers"
- patience and persistence to work with detail
- natural tendency toward orderliness
- ability to handle pressure in meeting deadlines
- decision-making skills
- computer and information sciences skills

Testing

If you are interested in finding out whether your personal aptitudes, skills, and interests would lead to success in an accounting program, look into the College Accounting Testing Program. This program includes four tests—an aptitude test, two levels of achievement tests, and a vocational interest inventory. It attempts to predict professional success, both in the college program and on the job. The test battery enables individual students and colleges to compare results with scores of other students and colleges on a national basis. For more information about this battery of tests, ask in the office of the accounting department of your college or write to:

AICPA Testing Project Office
1211 Avenue of the Americas
New York, NY 10036

The widest range of job opportunities in public accounting is offered to people who pass the Uniform CPA Examination, which is used in all states. The difficult, two-and-a-half day examination provides a challenge for those wanting to enter public accounting. Included in the exam are four sections in the areas of accounting practices, auditing standards, accounting theory, and business law. The failure rate is great on the CPA exam. Anyone who passes two sections with a minimum overall score may retake the other two at a later time. Those who do not achieve this minimum requirement must retake the entire exam. After successfully passing all parts of the exam, accountants may be eligible to receive the CPA certificate, which enables them to gain a permit to practice issued by their resident state board of accountancy. Many states require that individuals have one or two years of experience in accounting before receiving the CPA certificate. In 1990, eight states required that CPA candidates complete 150 semester hours of college education with a major in accounting, which suggests either a five-year bachelor's degree program or a master's degree. These factors contribute to restraining the growth in the number of certified public accountants.

SOURCES OF ADDITIONAL INFORMATION

If you like what you have read and would like more information on careers in accounting, write to the following professional organizations:

American Accounting
  Association
5717 Bessie Drive
Sarasota, FL 33583

American Association of
  Hispanic Certified Public
  Accountants
1414 Metropolitan Avenue
Bronx, NY 10462

This organization matches funds provided to needy students by local chapters.

American Institute of Certified
  Public Accountants
1211 Avenue of the Americas
New York, NY 10036-8775

This organization offers scholarships to minority accounting majors in both graduate and undergraduate programs.

American Society of Women
  Accountants
35 E. Wacker Drive, Suite 2250
Chicago, IL 60601

American Woman's Society of
  Certified Public Accountants
11 E. Wacker Drive, Suite 600
Chicago, IL 60601

Association of Government
  Accountants
601 Wythe Street, Suite 204
Alexandria, VA 22314

EDP Auditors Association
P.O. Box 88180
Carol Stream, IL 60188-0180

Institute of Internal Auditors,
  Inc.
249 Maitland Avenue, Box 1119
Altamonte Springs, FL
  32701-4201

National Association of
  Accountants
P. O. Box 433
10 Paragon Drive
Montvale, NJ 07645

National Association of Black
  Accountants
300 I Street N.E., Suite 107
Washington, DC 20002

National Society of Public
  Accountants
1010 N. Fairfax Street
Alexandria, VA 22314

This organization offers scholarships to those who have completed their sophomore year.

The American Assembly of Collegiate Schools of Business (AACSB) provides a list of accredited accounting and business programs. To obtain one, write:

AACSB
605 Old Ballas Road, Suite 220
St. Louis, MO 63141

Each state has a State Society of Certified Public Accountants as well as a State Board of Accountancy. The national association and address is as follows:

National Association of State
    Boards of Accountancy
545 Fifth Avenue
New York, NY 10017

CAREER DECISION-MAKING MODEL

Now that you have some information on careers in accounting in general, it is time to consider accounting as a possible career for you. Figure 2-2 is a form with the factors included from the career decision-making model in Chapter 1. Follow these directions in completing it.

1. Enter the position that interests you most on the line titled *Job*.
2. Enter any additional factors used to personalize your model (from Chapter 1) in the blank spaces provided.
3. Enter the weights that you assigned to the factors (from Chapter 1) in the column *WT*. (It would be wise to review the explanations of the factors in the description of the model in Chapter 1 before going on to step 4.)
4. Assign a value from 1 (lowest) to 10 (highest) to each factor based on the information in this chapter and on your personal self-assessment. (This value is different and separate from the weight.) Enter the value in column *V*. If you feel that you have a certain aptitude or attribute needed for success in this career area, you should assign a fairly high value. If a certain interest, such as amount of variety, is desirable to you and you feel the area provides the variety you enjoy, assign a fairly high value. If not, assign a low value. Use this technique to assign values to all factors in the model. If you cannot assign a value based on the information in the chapter for some of the factors in the model, either use other sources to acquire the information or leave the space beside the factor blank.
5. Multiply the weight times the value, entering the score in the column *S*.
6. Add the scores in column *S* for each group of factors, entering the number in the space labeled *Total*.

You will use this evaluation in Chapter 11 in combination with evaluations of each career explored in this book.

WHAT DID YOU LEARN?

In this chapter you learned a lot about careers in accounting. You now should understand such information as what services accountants provide, where they are employed, what salaries they earn, what mobility

Figure 2-2 Career evaluation for accounting

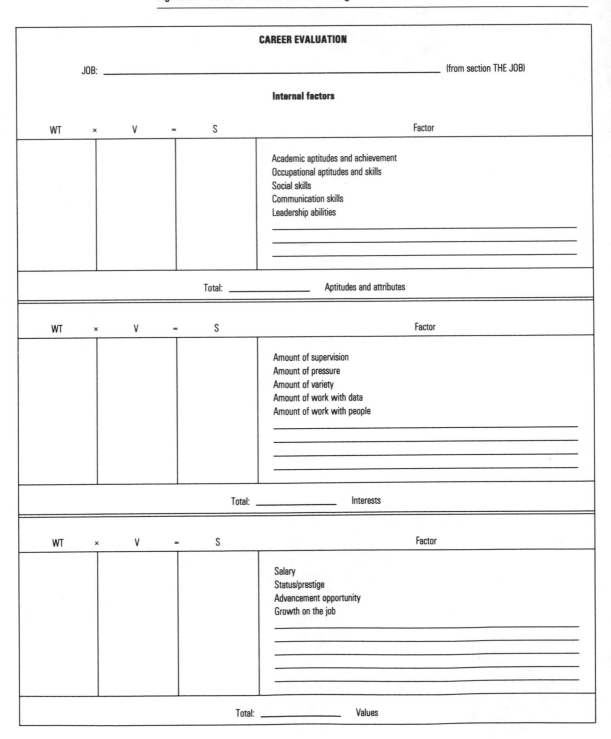

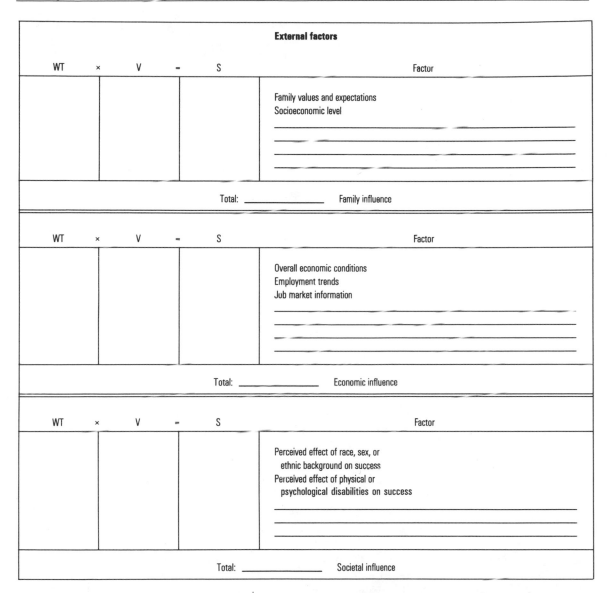

they have, what trends are currently affecting the profession, what the job outlook is, how to prepare yourself for a career in accounting, and where to write for additional information. You completed a career evaluation for accounting. In Chapter 3, "Careers in Computers and Information Technology," you will gain insights into careers in the exciting world of high technology.

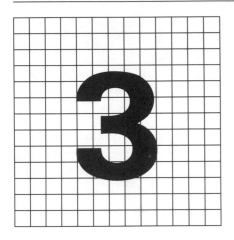

CAREERS IN COMPUTERS AND INFORMATION TECHNOLOGY

CHAPTER OBJECTIVES

Upon completion of this chapter, you should be able to:

1. Describe the work of computer professionals in systems development and programming, technical services and operations, the information center, information management, and computer design, manufacture, sales, and service.

2. Discuss trends in computers and information technology and their impact on careers.

3. Diagram career paths for those in computer and information careers.

4. Discuss job opportunities in computer and information fields today.

5. List the educational preparation and skills needed for positions in these fields.

6. Evaluate careers in computers and information technology according to your individualized career decision-making model.

Computers and information technology have dramatically changed the workplace. High-speed computers have enabled organizations in all industries to process vast quantities of data quickly. Organizations are able to offer more services to customers and employees, maintain better records, and obtain the vital information needed by management to make decisions that maximize profits and assure survival in a turbulent and competitive environment. The effect of the new technology has been to eliminate some jobs, to change others, and to create new ones. Many routine clerical jobs have been eliminated, creating in their place new, better-paid positions in the growing information systems field. On the other hand, the increased use of robots in industry has displaced many manufacturing workers. Jobs created through the expanded use of robots require technical skills not always easy for the unskilled or semi-skilled worker to obtain. Computerization requires retraining many people, adjusting to change (which is not easy), and filling new positions for which there are shortages of qualified individuals. Thus, there are both positive and negative aspects of the computer revolution. But to those entering the newer, better-paid positions born from computerization, it is easy to focus on the positive.

The development of the microprocessor created a revolution in computer usage. There are roughly 45 million personal computers in use in the United States today, 90 million worldwide. The computer has become a household word, if not an addition. Scenarios vary regarding how the computer will impact our lives in the future, just as individual life-styles vary, but one fact is certain—that computers will perform more mundane operations in our lives, saving us time and energy and increasing our possibilities for work and leisure. In terms of careers, the jobs of workers in practically every industry will be affected by the expanded use of computers. The increasing need for information suggests a promising future for computer and information professionals.

This chapter will enable you to examine careers in computers and information systems. It includes such information as

- what jobs computer and information professionals perform
- who employs these professionals
- salaries and career paths
- latest trends
- job opportunities
- education and skills needed to pursue computer careers
- sources of additional information on computers and information processing

THE JOB

The idea of computers in U.S. government work got its start with the use of newly invented card-sorting equipment in the compilation of the 1890 census. Today, massive data bases characterize many of the government's operations—for example, the modern Bureau of the Census and the Internal Revenue Service. Data base and information technology permeate all organizations today; computer and information professionals are employed in virtually every industry. Computers have been on the cutting edge of science and technology over the past few decades. The computer has been widely used for producing art, music, special effects in films, and the ever-popular video games. The computer has even made an impact in the sports arena. For example, the National Football League teams use computers to provide instant data on offensive and defensive plays of both a team and its opponent. Computers have been used for years in crime detection. Data base systems provide information on criminals, stolen vehicles, and missing persons.

These computer applications are but a few that demonstrate how the computer has advanced from its early clerical uses to extend across many fields. Computer professionals are directly responsible for some of the exciting outcomes described above. With the coming of the second computer age, there are now computers that seem to reason, make judgments, and learn. Such *artificial intelligence* enables computers to diagnose diseases, locate mineral deposits, determine where to drill oil wells, prepare income tax returns, give investment advice, and perform a variety of other "thinking" activities. Tomorrow's developments promise to be even more interesting than today's as advancing technology continues to exceed everyone's expectations.

Computers are used at every level of most organizations. From management decision making to simple recordkeeping, billing, payroll, and inventory control applications, computers play a valuable role in businesses. Science labs use computers in research. Automated equipment is common in manufacturing plants. Executives are rarely without their desktop computers as they call up the information required to make complicated and crucial decisions. In grocery stores and other retail outlets, computerized scanners enable quicker service and better inventory control. The banking and airline industries have been computer-dependent in almost every aspect of their operations for years.

Computer professionals may be employed in a variety of jobs by almost any type of organization or within the computer industry itself. The types of jobs held by computer professionals in most organizations fall into the following general categories: systems development and programming, technical services and operations, the information center, and information systems management. Figure 3-1 uses key management positions to show how the information function may be organized. Jobs in the computer industry include all of these areas plus jobs in computer design, manufacture, sales, and service.

Systems Development and Programming

The area of systems development and programming includes many jobs, such as *systems analyst* and *programmer*. These jobs involve the development of systems including sets of instructions—called software—to serve a variety of purposes in business, science, entertainment, and other fields. Software may be produced by computer vendors and sold along with the hardware, or it may be produced in-house, in both cases by computer professionals in systems development and programming.

Systems analyst. The work of the systems analyst is to design a new system or to improve an existing one. A system is a collection of people, machines, programs, and procedures organized to perform a certain task. Basically a professional problem solver, the systems analyst must first analyze problems or informational needs within the organization, then design efficient patterns of information flows from the data sources to the computer to solve them. The systems analyst also plans the distribution of information, based on how it is to be used within the organization. In order to design and maintain a reliable and efficient system of information flows, the systems analyst works closely, often in teams, with managers, accountants, and other user groups within the organization to determine their informational needs or problems. An understanding of how various areas in the organization operate, such as accounting and marketing, and the ability to communicate effectively

Figure 3-1 Information Organization Chart

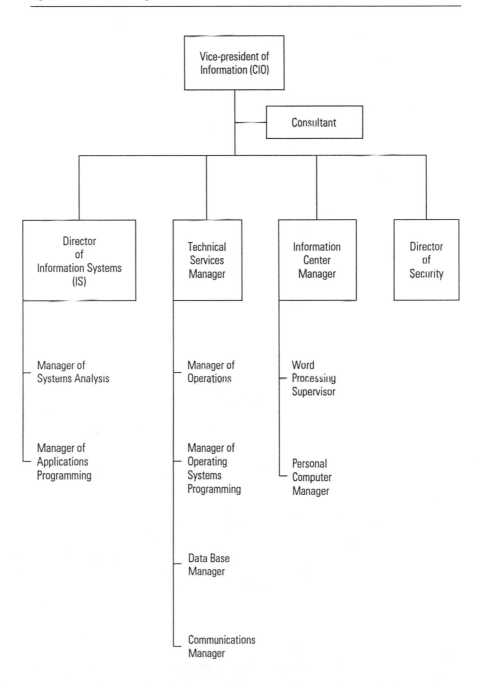

with coworkers in these areas are crucial to the effectiveness of the systems analyst.

Most systems analysts have some supervisory or management duties such as estimating, scheduling, controlling time, and accepting final responsibility for projects. An important part of the systems analyst's job is to relate the requirements of the system to the capabilities of the computer hardware and prepare specifications for programmers to follow in developing the software to make the system work. In some organizations, the systems analyst also may do the programming and hold the job title *analyst/programmer*. In other organizations, analysts and programmers have separate job titles and areas of responsibility. Most analysts begin their careers as programmers.

Programmer. The work of the computer programmer involves coding—that is, writing detailed sets of instructions according to the problem descriptions and specifications of the systems analysts. These programs are made up of a series of logical steps for the machine to follow to process the data into usable information. The programmer may use any one of over 1,000 programming languages; COBOL, FORTRAN, Pascal, and BASIC are among the older, more common languages. In programming, a strong orientation to detail is important in that something as small as a misplaced comma could cause the program to malfunction. This characteristic becomes crucial as a programmer *debugs* his or her programs to ensure that they are error-free. Debugging usually entails making trial runs on the computer with sample data. Programmers may also be involved in writing documentation or instructions that explain how to use the software. Often technical writers are employed to prepare the documentation according to instructions prepared by the programmers. Programs may be written in a matter of hours or may require more than a year of work; thus programmers may work alone on small projects or in teams on larger ones.

There are several types of programmers: scientific and business applications programmers, operating systems programmers, and maintenance programmers. The work of *scientific, or engineering, applications programmers* is highly mathematical in nature and involves developing programs that solve scientific or engineering problems. Normally an undergraduate degree in engineering, math, or science is a minimum requirement. Some background in FORTRAN, Pascal, Assembler, or C Programming languages is necessary. Also desirable are a master of science degree, large-scale and personal hardware exposure, and operating systems programming experience.

Business applications programmers are involved in a wide range of tasks, from developing user programs to handling such routine activities as billing customers. They also may develop programs designed to satisfy the complex informational needs of managers. Programming experience pays off in landing desirable jobs if it is pertinent to the systems in use in a particular company. The improved quality and quantity of software packages in business applications has reduced the demand for business application programmers somewhat. However, the widespread use of personal computers has created a strong demand for programmers experienced in BASIC, FORTRAN RPG II, and Pascal on small commercial systems. Besides developing applications programs, personal computer programmers also support such functions as communications, graphics, data base, or operating systems.

Maintenance programmers are employed to constantly enhance or debug existing major programs. Skill in debugging techniques and experience in program development are required for this highly complex job. The maintenance programming staff is usually a combination of seasoned veterans and newly hired programmers who are trained by the most experienced maintenance programmers on the staff.

The work of *operating systems programmers* is highly technical in nature and somewhat difficult for the layperson to understand. Basically, the operating systems programmer writes sets of instructions to make the programming of computers easier, for example, programs that schedule the various components of the computer or that permit the computer to deal with many tasks simultaneously. These sets of instructions, called operating systems, control the operation of the entire computer system. They frequently become a permanent part of the computer's memory so that all of the components and related equipment perform in harmony with one another. Thus, the operating systems programmer must have a good technical knowledge of the parts of the computer and how they operate. Systems programmers might be involved in developing new languages or adapting existing languages to specific needs. A degree in computer science with a solid background in computer architecture (the way circuits are structured) is required for most positions along with some experience with Assembler language programming.

Applications and maintenance programmers normally work under the *director of information systems*, while operating systems programmers work under the *technical services manager*, as can be seen in the chart in Figure 3-1.

Technical Services and Operations

One of the major information departments in an organization, technical services consists of managers, systems analysts, operating systems programmers, and specialists in data base and data communications technologies. A *technical services manager* heads this department.

A data base is a set of related data used by systems analysts and programmers to produce the information needed by the organization. *Data base administrators* analyze the company's information requirements, coordinate data collection, organize data into usable data bases, store data for efficient access by analysts and programmers, keep data bases up-to-date, and establish rules pertaining to the data bases and their security. Working under the administrators to assist in these tasks are *data base analysts* and *librarians*.

Data communications or telecommunications involves the use of hardware and software to link a computer to remote terminals and other computers. The *data communications manager* and the analysts working under the manager are responsible for the design of data communications networks and the installation and operation of data links. Data communications specialists must be knowledgeable in languages, applications, and communications devices. They are responsible for program design, coding, testing, debugging, documentation, and implementation of communications software. Their work also involves the evaluation and modification of existing communications hardware and software.

The *manager of operations* oversees computer operators who are responsible for setting up the computer and its equipment; mounting and removing tapes, disks, and printer forms; monitoring jobs in progress; and troubleshooting when problems occur. *Data entry operators* are involved in input—that is, entering data into the computer using keyboards and tape or disks. *Production control operators* handle output, routing jobs to the proper place upon completion. Most positions in operations require training that may be obtained in high school, vocational school, community college, or on the job. While entry into these jobs requires a minimum of formal education, advancement is very limited.

The Information Center

The information center offers still more employment possibilities for individuals with keyboard proficiency and a minimum of formal training. This center is a clearinghouse where needed documents are generated and routed to proper departments within the company. Word processing personnel perform these duties and may advance within the center from the position of trainee to supervisor. A *data processing manager* heads the department. *Data entry and word processing operators* are workers with a tolerance for routine duties. The word processing field is changing somewhat as a result of the explosion in use of personal computers and new workstation networks.

Increasing numbers of workers outside the information center are using personal computers for information and word processing. A new position—*personal computer user services specialist*—was created to provide support and to coordinate the use of personal computers throughout the company. Personal computer user specialists work with systems development and management information systems professionals as well as with user groups from functional areas throughout the organization. Integrating and directing the use of personal computers to analyze informational needs and coordinate office automation efforts are an important part of the job. In addition, user specialists conduct training in the use of personal computers. Excellent communications skills as well as personal computer knowledge are requisites for this job. In large organizations, personal computer user specialists work directly under a *personal computer manager*.

Information Systems Management

Throughout all of the areas previously described are *information systems (IS) managers* working at various levels within their departments. The key management positions are shown in Figure 3-1. Today, there are fewer levels of middle managers in corporations, partly as a result of new communications technologies. Upper-level managers can obtain higher quality and timelier information directly from the computer than was supplied to them by middle managers in the past. IS managers must have both technical and managerial skills. The higher the level of management, the more important managerial skills become. The lower the level, the more vital technical expertise is, since it is the systems analysts, programmers, data base administrators, and communications professionals who work on the cutting edge of new technology. In fact, many information professionals refuse management positions so that they may continue to work closely with technology.

Basically, managers at all levels are involved with planning, budgeting, hiring, scheduling, supervising, evaluating performance, and many other tasks. The buck stops with department and other managers who have authority over various operations. Those who successfully move up the ranks to the highest levels of information management possess excellent decision-making and communications skills, an understanding of business and the management style of the company, and the ability to work well with people and to command their respect. With greater emphasis being placed on management information systems and decision support systems, information managers are rising to top-level positions in organizations.

Assisting information mangers are both *internal and external consultants*, who keep up with the latest technological advances and how to integrate them into the organization to keep it competitive. You will learn more about a career in consulting in Chapter 10. Another computer professional important in many organizations today is the *director of security*. With greater computer usage and access have come serious problems, such as crime, fraud, privacy invasion, and even computer viruses deliberately implanted in systems or software to cause mischief or havoc. Computer security may be maintained by an in-house team or by external teams of computer security specialists, sometimes called *tiger teams*. These teams conduct periodic, often unscheduled, security checks on systems at the request of management to detect existing and potential problems.

Computer Design, Manufacture, Sales, and Service

Employed by computer manufacturers in addition to the computer professionals previously described are the scientists, mathematicians, engineers, and technicians who research, design and produce the *hardware* (equipment) and the *software* (programs) to make it work. The equipment is designed by *hardware engineers* with electrical or electronics backgrounds who specialize in computer engineering. The systems analysts and programmers who design the software are called *software engineers* within the computer industry. Once the hardware and software is developed, it is marketed by a *sales representative*—an individual specializing in business systems or scientific applications. Once the system is sold, the *field engineer* installs the hardware and software and services it periodically to keep it running smoothly. The *service representative* helps solve day-to-day problems and is usually knowledgeable in both computer programming and the technical aspects of computers. From either a sales or a service rep position, an individual is upwardly mobile and can aspire to management levels.

Data service organizations employ systems analysts, programmers, computer and data entry operators, and sales and service representatives. These organizations process data for customers who do not maintain computer systems or need additional capacity. More and more companies are using data service organizations rather than purchasing equipment that may be technologically obsolete in a short time. In addition to data processing, many of these companies provide professional services as well, including systems analysis and design, documentation, and employee training.

CAREER PATHS AND COMPENSATION

Most entry-level job applicants in computer and information professions find positions with insurance companies, banks, computer manufacturing firms, data service firms, major research labs, and government. A premium is placed on the right kind of knowledge and experience. Supply and demand play an important part in career mobility and salary. The more in demand the particular area of specialization, the more mobility an individual has and the higher salary he or she earns.

Salaries

Overall, the salary picture for computer careers is positive. Salaries of top-level and entry-level workers have increased steadily over the past three years, by 20 and 25 percent, respectively. Managers of systems analysis and applications programming have increased their salaries, on average, 11 to 12 percent over the same time period. Communications managers gained 16.4 percent over the past three years, and data-base managers' salaries rose at a higher rate than systems analysis and programming managers as well, with a gain of 25 percent just from 1988 to 1989. The big losers have been operating systems programmers and managers, with small declines in some salaries in computer operations and systems analysis/programming positions as well.

A number of factors affect salaries of computer professionals. It has become harder and harder to generalize about salaries, but usually the larger the information systems budget, the higher the salaries of the computer professionals. Also, the higher the company revenues, the higher the salaries. Two other factors affect the salary picture—industry and geography—but these vary somewhat with each position. Technology-oriented industries usually offer higher salaries to individuals in technical areas. Geography affects salaries; the highest salaries are offered in cities and areas of the country where the cost-of-living differences are the highest.

Other Factors

Salary is not the only factor important to computer professionals. It may not be the most important factor in many cases. Such factors as the challenge of being on the cutting edge, the opportunity to use new technology, a humanistic managerial style, and promotion from within with no barriers all have great appeal. Training and career development are vital to information professionals if they are to stay in touch technically and advance. In past years, when the programmer shortage was greatest, employers actually chose not to provide much training, believing that the more highly trained their individuals, the more likely it was that they would be hired away by other firms. This was an ineffective tactic because of the high growth need of computer professionals, who were then forced to change jobs to keep current. Both individuals who remained in low-growth positions and their employers now realize how lack of training reduces productivity.

Not surprisingly, the industry offering the highest salaries to computer professionals is the computer industry. Salary only partially explains the lure of the computer industry. Computer vendors are able to attract qualified people because of excellent benefit packages, training programs, and continued industry growth forecasts. Many IS managers feel that computer vendors offer greater job security. Loss of jobs through company adoption of new technologies or mergers, which is occurring across all industries, has become a large threat to many IS managers. In addition, one of the fastest ways to achieve high salary status is through computer sales. Computer sales representatives with one or two years of experience earn from $45,000 to $80,000 a year. Data services sales representatives can earn from $50,000 to $70,000 per year.

Advancement

As you have seen, computer professionals are employed in a variety of positions in organizations. How these positions are organized or how many specialized positions exist depends on the philosophy and size of the organization, the technological orientation of the company, or the industry norms. More opportunities for advancement as well as employment rest with the larger organizations. Many have professional training facilities available to entry-level personnel. Some firms have dual-career ladders, which provide training in both management and technical skills. There are more position openings to which you can advance in a larger firm, and many firms promote from within. On the other hand, small firms often offer a wider variety of work experiences in one position, a greater possibility of entering a management position early in one's career, and continued involvement in technical areas even though a move into management is made. This last advantage is worth considering. Jumping too quickly into management and leaving the technical front could render one's knowledge obsolete in a short time because of continuous technological advancement. This poses the greatest dilemma for IS managers, since mobility is greatly limited for those who fail to keep abreast of the changes.

Figure 3-2 indicates various information positions in a large organization, the patterns of mobility, and the salary ranges. Figure 3-2 is a standard organizational chart. The areas of systems development and technical services include numerous specialists. You can see from the chart the levels at which individuals work at different stages of their career development and how individuals with different functions work together. These systems development, technical services, and information center professionals comprise the information function in an organization.

CURRENT TRENDS

While technological innovations have continued beyond even futurists' wildest dreams over the past decade, state-of-the-art computer technology has realized only a fraction of its potential. The dilemma is how to transfer technology from the research-and-development lab to a development team and finally into the hands of users. Many experts feel that the next 10 years will be characterized by better use of existing technologies rather than by technological breakthroughs. The new technologies introduced in the 1980s that will shape computing and impact computer careers in the 1990s include improved personal computer and workstation technologies, expert systems in the area of artificial intelligence, local area networks (LANS) in the field of communications, computer-aided software engineering (CASE), and imaging systems in the field of optical technology.

Personal Computers

Over the 1980s, improvements in personal computer technology caused an explosion in their numbers and uses. Personal computers became smaller, with laptop sales growing at twice the rate of desktop personal computers. By the mid-1990s, powerful computers will fit in briefcases. The power of the personal computer has grown, rivaling the more powerful workstations, which are enhanced microcomputers with stand-alone, communications, and electronic mail capabilities as well. The trend is toward ever-smaller, yet more powerful, personal computers—and the technology is in place. Today's fastest desktop computers run at 5 to 10 MIPS (millions of instructions per second). In 10 years, it is esti-

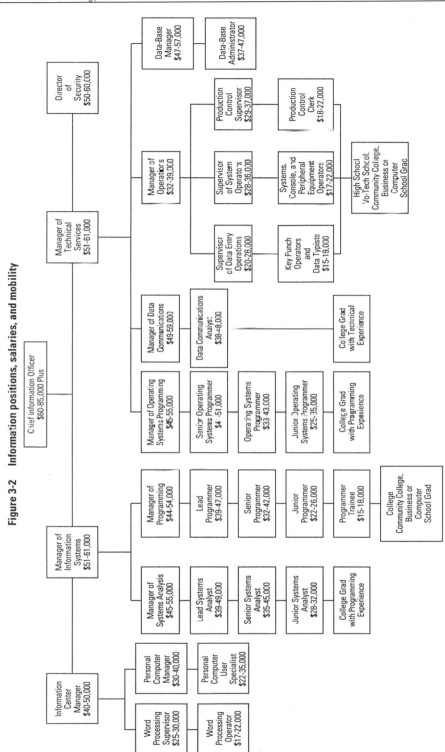

Figure 3-2   Information positions, salaries, and mobility

mated that desktop computers will be capable of 1 billion instructions per second. Software development has begun to catch up with the hardware, offering an ever-wider variety of applications and competing products.

The increase in personal computer use in organizations has given birth to a new job, the *personal computer manager*. Companies providing technology and professional services have aggressive goals to acquire one personal computer for every employee, or total saturation by the mid-1990s. The increased number of computer users has resulted in greater demand for personal computer user specialists, analysts, and programmers.

Expert Systems

Despite the skeptical reception a few years ago of artificial intelligence, such diverse industries as utilities, chemicals, transportation, electronics, health care, and process manufacturing are developing and using *expert systems*. These systems are designed to simulate thinking of experts in the field to provide "intelligent" information to be used in decision making. As always, the limits of the new technology were misunderstood initially. The expert system is designed not to replace, but rather to assist, the expert. Physicians use expert systems to match signs and symptoms, suggest diagnoses, and provide information on drugs. Railroads are developing expert systems to perform better derailment and accident analysis modeling. Utility companies are using expert systems to determine when to purchase the oil, gas, and uranium for electricity production. Almost every industry can offer examples of expert systems development or use.

The delay in the introduction of expert systems is due in part to the lack of individuals in systems analysis and programming who possess the skills to produce such systems. These computer professionals, called *knowledge engineers*, are among the most wanted by corporations today.

Communications

The field of communications has had a dramatic effect on computer technology. Banks, airlines, retail stores, and numerous other consumer industries use computer terminals for *on-line transaction-processing* (OLTP). The electronic pathways that connect these terminals with a central or main computer is called a *network*. A network covering a broad geographical area is called a *wide area network* (WAN). A network confined to one building or office complex is called a *local area network* (LAN). More widespread use of personal computers has greatly contributed to the establishment of LANs. Networks of the future will link together PCs, minicomputers, and mainframes, giving users access to vast information sources.

Initially, personal computers were used by individuals alone to increase their personal productivity. As more people within a company got personal computers, the desire to use them to communicate with each other electronically arose. Thus the concept of *electronic mail* began to be used internally. It was far easier and quicker to send a memo electronically through the *LAN* than through the office mail. In addition, personal computers can be connected to the main computer, printers, and copy machines for direct access to data files and equipment housed in a central place in the building. Thus LANs provide a more efficient and productive way for company employees to perform their jobs, share information, and communicate throughout the organization without ever leaving their offices. Such office computer networks have created a demand for a new type of software called "groupware" to improve communications and coordinate work activities. Advances in communications technology will provide, probably within this decade, LANs of multimedia workstations that allow transmission of not only print and graphics, but also voice, video, and even three-dimensional animated digital graphics.

CASE Tools

Computer-aided Software Engineering (CASE) tools are software packages used to generate code according to parameters specified by programmers. CASE tools can greatly reduce the time required by programmers to generate new programs and to revise old ones. The greatest cost in information systems is in programming because of the time required to write and debug programs. For this reason, many companies began to use independent contractors to develop programs or packaged software. Off-the-shelf software does not always work well for highly specific applications and must still be modified to serve the company's purposes. The new CASE tools enable organizations to once again develop their own software without the tremendous cost and time commitments of the past.

While CASE tools do not eliminate the job of the programmer in most cases, they do modify it and reduce programmer time, which could in large operations eliminate programmer jobs. In time as the tools are improved and become more user-friendly, individuals other than programmers may be able to generate programs without formal training in programming. The demand for application programmers already has declined as the software industry continues to produce more and better software packages. If the potential of CASE tools is realized, this decline will be even greater. On the other hand, there will be many opportunities within the software industry itself for programmers with the skills to produce state-of-the-art programs.

Imaging Systems

Banking, insurance, transportation, health care, and petroleum industries are enthusiastic about the advances in imaging systems. These systems enable documents to be digitized and shared across large networks.

Faster and easier retrieval of documents in paper-intensive industries provides the key to efficiency. The associated area of optical storage reduces the space required to house company records. Optical disks and other high-density storage devices are also more convenient to access than microfilm and microfiche. Like the other new technologies, imaging systems and optical storage have great potential. A *gigabyte* is roughly equivalent to the amount of material contained in 700 books with an average of 400 pages each, not counting pictures. It is estimated that within five years, a storage device containing a gigabyte of data will fit in a shirt pocket. Specialists with expertise in imaging systems will find many new job opportunities in the future.

Information Systems

Information systems directors are overwhelmed by the variety of new products on the market. To be competitive, a company must be as productive as the competition is. Information systems can provide the means for improved productivity. To lag behind technologically is to lose one's competitive edge. The problem is to select the best tools to make use of the new technologies. For this reason many companies form *advanced technology groups* (ATGs), or teams of people assigned the task of studying the new technologies and recommending the best ways to implement them in the organization. The decisions made by information managers affect the roles of computer professionals within their organizations.

Computers are the tools that generate information, but information is the resource that is shaping the future. In corporations today, the emphasis is on information services rather than on computer systems. This move from the technical to the applied has changed the nature and title of many jobs, the demand for certain skills, and the very terminology of the field. Information systems (IS) has replaced data processing (DP) to show the broader scope of both computer technology and applications.

JOB OPPORTUNITIES

An analysis of job market figures for computer careers yields a positive picture for most computer professionals. Though demand for workers in most areas will grow, closer scrutiny is advisable for several reasons: demand is not increasing uniformly in all areas; there is a declining demand in some; areas of specialization are changing as technology changes.

Demand

A number of factors influence the demand for information professionals. A dramatic increase in the number of computer systems in use today has been a bonanza for the computer industry. Numerous surveys put electrical engineers and computer science graduates at the top of the

Table 3-1 Fastest Growing Occupations from 1986 to 2000

Occupation	1986	2000	% Change
Computer equipment repairers	69,000	125,000	80.4
Computer systems analysts	331,000	582,000	75.6
Computer programmers	479,000	813,000	69.9
Operations and systems researchers	38,000	59,000	54.1
Peripheral equipment operators	46,000	70,000	50.8
Data entry keyers, composing	29,000	43,000	50.8

Source: Bureau of Labor Statistics

most-wanted lists, along with chemical engineers. Although the computer manufacturing industry is one of the fastest-growing in the economy, its rate of growth will slow down compared to its explosive growth in the past. Demand for computers will continue to increase with expanding purchases by individual consumers. More than 25 percent of the jobs in computer manufacturing are for engineers, technicians, and systems analysts. Production workers represent only 35 percent, compared to the 68 percent in manufacturing as a whole. Projected employment figures in the computer manufacturing industry show an increase from 85,000 jobs in 1986 to 503,000 in 2000. The shift in emphasis from production to research and development will continue since new product development is the key growth factor.

Computers now are used in many industries, and new applications are being developed constantly. Advances in both hardware and software enable the user to have more computer capability per investment dollar. The computer has become an irresistible tool still very much in demand. Along with the demand for more computer hardware and software comes the demand for people to produce and use it, both inside and outside computer-related industries.

Growth in the demand for computer professionals will continue through the year 2000. Bureau of Labor Statistics figures indicate that computer careers are among the fastest-growing. Table 3-1 indicates growth in numbers and percentages for selected occupations.

Over half of the new job openings for systems analysts and computer programmers are predicted to occur in the computer and data services industries. Despite the new, more effective programming tools, a variety of new applications will assure the new jobs for programmers. Remember that demand is declining for operating systems programmers, so the chosen area of specialization is an important consideration. Among engineers, electrical engineers will gain 192,000 jobs, a 48 percent increase from 1986 to 2000. Most of the increase in these positions will occur in the industries of communications equipment, computers, and other electronic equipment. Opportunities for electrical and electronic technicians will increase substantially as well.

Declines are predicted in a number of clerical occupations as a result of new office automation and technological changes. Typists and word processors will decline in numbers by 14 percent and data entry keyers, except composing, by 16 percent. (Data entry keyers who actually compose reports and other documents will be in great demand. Composition requires knowledge of a specific area and writing skills.) Also declining a little or remaining the same as a result of factory automation will be jobs for electrical and electronic equipment assemblers.

Along with the demand of particular industries, trends pinpointing the demand for specific areas of expertise can be summarized as follows. The increasing popularity of the personal computer has dramatically increased demand for those who can design, build, and develop software for them. Both individual consumers and companies will buy personal computers in increasing numbers. Personal computer user specialists and managers will be in demand by companies. Contributing to this demand will be more widespread use of network technologies. Specialists in communications and data-base technologies will be sought by every industry. Systems analysts and applications programmers with expertise in these areas as well as in expert systems, systems integration, and image processing will be very much in demand. Growth will continue in the fields of computer-aided design and manufacturing. More jobs will be created in the robotics industry. Office automation is firmly established, and electronic mail has become as familiar as the daily postal carrier. Individuals with skills on specific types of equipment will be in demand.

Supply

Demand is half of the job market picture; supply is the other half. Opportunities will continue to be abundant for computer professionals because supply will not keep pace with demand in most areas, particularly for entry-level workers. As demand grows, a percentage decline will continue in the young adult population between the ages of 16 and 24 from 30 percent of the labor force in 1985 to 16 percent in the year 2000. With competition from business, universities, and the military, there will not be enough young entry-level workers to go around.

A smaller entry-level labor force means a reduced supply of information personnel who are already in demand. Entry-level systems analysts and applications programmers educated in the new technologies will be able to pick and choose. Overall interest of college freshmen in computer careers declined from 8.8 percent in 1982 to 2.2 percent in 1987. However, as more business-oriented information systems programs are developed, more interest will be generated. To compensate for the supply-and-demand gap, companies are attempting to build systems and organizations requiring fewer people, increase training efforts, and develop more attractive compensation packages to lure the young talent.

This bright picture for young, entry-level personnel has a more somber side for older workers. Promotions will continue to be more competitive because of larger numbers of middle-aged workers with obsolete skills, the need to staff lower-level jobs, and the current trend to reduce middle management positions. Most older workers have neither the skills nor the inclination to postpone retirement to build system architectures.

Working at home

Opportunities to work in information careers exist both in companies and at home. At-home terminals and personal computers make it possible for those who can work only at home to hold a job and receive a competitive salary for doing it. Apart from the millions of Americans who work full-time for companies and bring work home from time to time, there are three major categories of those who work at home:

1. Entrepreneurs who run small businesses from their homes.
2. Home-based employees who are electronically linked to the company office (telecommuters).
3. Independent contractors.

Of the estimated 25 million home-office workers, about half are women and about 6 million are self-employed women. Women comprise about 70 percent of all home-based sole proprietorships. The breakdown of all people working from home is as follows:

- 50 percent in professional or managerial occupations
- 33 percent in sales, technical, or administrative fields
- 17 percent in precision production, repair, and other assorted fields

Information-related service jobs will dominate home-office work. While home-based workers are a small minority in business, it has been projected that by 1993 their numbers will rise to roughly 34.8 million.

The personal computer, with its user-friendly operation, affordable prices, and variety of software has been the driving force behind this trend. Several economic factors contribute to the growth in home-based work. Individuals laid off or retired early often start home-based businesses. Women (or men) with child-care responsibilities find working at home an alternative to expensive day-care centers and a way to spend more time with their children. Corporations can save money on office space and workplace maintenance using telecommuters and independent contractors.

Sources of information for home-based workers include:

American Home Business
Association
397 Post Road
Darien, CT 06820
1-800-433-6361

National Association for the
  Self-Employed
P.O. Box 612067
Dallas, TX 75261
1-800-232-6273

American Business Management
13470 Washington Blvd.
Marina del Ray, CA 90292
(231) 306-1776

The following publications are available for purchase:

The Business Plan for
  Home-Based Businesses
SBA Publications
P.O. Box 30
Denver, CO 80201-0030
Cost: $1.00

Home Office Computing
730 Broadway
New York, NY 10003
A monthly magazine, annual
  subscription rate: $19.97

Numerous books on home-based businesses are available in your local library.

Temporary service agencies

In addition to working at home, temporary services offer an alternative to full-time permanent positions at offices. Temporary service firms have expanded from offering low-skill workers for emergency fill-in positions to workers with personal computer skills who may be hired routinely to meet business fluctuations or to complete an entire project headed by a temporary manager. Automation skills make up roughly a fourth of the business of temporary service firms. Demand has increased for PC programmers and consultants. These individuals earn between $35 and $50 per hour, depending on experience.

Equal opportunity standing

One of the most exciting and positive aspects of computer careers is that not only are there opportunities for so many meaningful careers, but everyone has a chance at them without being subjected to as many traditional biases regarding sex, race, national origin, age, sexual orientation, marital status, and other personal characteristics. This is not to say that placement in computer careers is free from any of this type of discrimination. But because of a number of factors, this discrimination is far less than in most other career areas.

One factor that has contributed to a positive record for employing women and members of racial or ethnic minorities is that the computer field is a relatively new one. Its growth has occurred concurrently with many consciousness-raising activities in the area of equal employment opportunity, such as the development of the women's movement and the Equal Employment Opportunity Commission. Another factor is the demand for skilled personnel in rapidly growing computer fields. In the past, managers were not in a position to overlook the talent of women and minorities—they had to focus on getting enough qualified people to do the job regardless of their personal characteristics. Given those opportunities, women have risen to key positions in information fields, further contributing to equal opportunities for women at all levels. Women have organized their own professional organizations.

As is the case with women, the computer marketplace has done a better job of hiring minority candidates than have other fields. Asian Americans have been highly successful. The number of key positions they hold is very high in proportion to their overall representation in the industry. Hispanics have also done very well. Although African Americans have been somewhat underrepresented in the past, this inequity is lessening as those who have entered computer fields gain experience and help recruit other African Americans. Emphasis on the development of math skills with youths is needed.

Many of the qualities that members of minority groups need for success are rarely taught in schools. Such business sense as how to set priorities is important. Determining what is important to the organization—that is, how it makes its money—is essential. Good communication and leadership skills are also important. These qualities, in combination with five years of technical experience, have earmarked many minority members for management positions in larger organizations as well as in their own companies.

Because computer programming is an activity that engages the mind rather than the body, it has been a very promising career for the physically disabled. In addition, computer technology has enabled the disabled and homebound to work in a number of other fields as well, such as accounting, bookkeeping, and other fields that permit outside contact via telephone, telefacsimile, and computer terminal. Microprocessors and minicomputers are being used to control the operation of typewriters, tape recorders, telephones, television, lighting, appliances, wheelchairs, limb prostheses, and manipulators. The research and training center of the National Institute of Handicapped Research has developed an entire office environment that can be run by a quadriplegic using a computer-controlled system.

Tax credits are offered to employers hiring the socially handicapped. For example, convicted felons who received data processing skills in such prisons as San Quentin, Leavenworth, and Terre Haute are now out of jail and contributing to society.

A Handicapped Educational Exchange (HEX) service provides up-to-date information concerning the education of and communications with the handicapped. For more information, write:

HEX
11523 Charlton Drive
Silver Spring, MD 20902

A free quarterly newsletter can be obtained by writing to:

Computer-Disability News
National Easter Seal
Society
2023 W. Ogden Avenue
Chicago, IL 60612

The computer industry has fewer age-related biases than most. The generation that is growing up with computers is also growing wealthier with them. Young entrepreneurs ages 12 to 20 are turning their command of computer programming into sizable profits by writing software. Their imagination and enthusiasm have given them the edge over work-weary, time-constrained adults in the development of games. In past years, talented teens have earned royalties in six-digit figures for developing popular games. The demand for these games has increased every year, making electronic games one of the fast growing segments in the computer industry.

The elderly are not to be excluded from computer career opportunities, either. Eric Knudson began his software company, ACS America, Inc., to capitalize on the work ethic of retired senior citizens and their talents. Knudson developed training centers and recruited workers 55 years old or older. If able to pass a programming aptitude test, the applicant was given three months free training and hired by ACS America as a subcontractor. These subcontractors are not given such fringe benefits as health or life insurance, but most already have those from Medicare and previous employers. What the retirees gain is a new skill, a way to make extra money, and a productive way to spend their time. Opportunities abound for older workers in temporary service firms. Kelly Services has begun the ENCORE program to attract older workers and retirees to temporary service jobs. Information kits are distributed to organizations for retirees and seniors outlining the advantages of temporary work.

The message of this section is that anyone who has the ability to do the job can find meaningful work in computer careers, both inside and outside the home. As long as demand remains high, these opportunities are likely to continue.

APTITUDES AND ATTRIBUTES NEEDED FOR SUCCESS

In response to the demand for skilled computer professionals, numerous educational programs are available in every state. Depending on an individual's career goal, the required background may be gained in a high school, vocational school, data processing school, community college, college, or university. Educational requirements have been discussed as part of the specific job descriptions in this chapter, so this section will focus on where to obtain the needed education and training.

Education

Children today are exposed to computers in preschools as early as two years old. New electronic learning aids help students become comfortable with the new technology. More elementary and secondary schools arc offering computer courses—not only computer literacy courses, but also programming and word processing at the high school level. The first programming course is often a good determinant of whether an individual has an aptitude and a strong enough interest to pursue an information processing career. Often performance in a programming course is a better indicator of aptitude and interest than a data processing aptitude test. The sooner the exposure to computers, the better. Since knowing how to use a computer is valuable in any career, every student who can afford a computer should buy one—the sooner, the better. There are many manufacturer-sponsored discount programs, often accompanied by free introductory courses in how to use them. Early exposure to computers is helpful, but success in educational programs in computer and information fields depends on strong basic skills in language and math.

Vocational and technical schools offer a variety of programs for those interested in data entry, operations, maintenance, service, electronics, programming, and so on. Usually, specialized data processing schools offer programs in these areas as well. At the community college, one-year or two-year programs in data entry, programming, or computer operations are usually offered. Often credits can be transferred to a college offering four-year degree programs. Employers may pay for the additional education. The majority of the careers discussed in this book require college and university degrees and, in some cases, graduate study.

Information majors are usually able to find internships or cooperative education (co-op) positions. Traditional internships were three-month summer positions while co-op programs were six months or longer. Internships usually were arranged by an interested faculty member and a company manager, and the intern was not always paid. Co-ops, on the other hand, were part of an ongoing college program for which students received both credits and pay. These distinctions aren't as clear any more, since companies want interns for longer periods as well and pay frequently is offered. Today, an estimated 250,000 students hold co-op positions in roughly 50,000 organizations, with students in IS management among the greatest in demand. Students earn wages and gain invaluable experience. Many organizations later hire their brightest interns and co-op students for full-time jobs. Apart from these programs, many students with computer skills find part-time jobs on their own that offer both pay and experience.

Training
Training is the most important ingredient in the success formula for computer professionals. It is the lack of good training and development opportunities that causes individuals to become dead-ended early in their careers. The first question that a job applicant should ask is, "What kind of training and development will the company provide me if I accept this position?"

The recent emphasis on training is due in part to the failure of college curricula in computer and information sciences to educate graduates in the high-demand skill areas. Dramatic changes in technology and organizational structure require constant educational program evaluation and modification. Curriculum change occurs too slowly. Along with the companies specializing in training services, major computer vendors such as IBM and Wang offer seminars and institutes for all technical levels. Training opportunities are also available to members through their professional organizations.

Certification
The Institute of Certification of Computer Professionals (ICCP) is a nonprofit organization that tests and certifies computer programmers and data processing managers. The certification process is a coordinated, industrywide effort to promote higher standards of performance. Currently, there are two major certification programs:

1. *The Certificate in Data Processing (CDP)* is primarily for business-oriented data processing people at supervisory and management levels. The half-day examination contains five sections: (1) data processing equipment, (2) computer programming and software, (3) principles of management, (4) accounting and quantitative methods, and (5) systems analysis and design.

2. *The Certificate in Computer Programming (CCP)* is primarily for senior-level programmers. The examination for this certificate consists of a general portion taken by all programmers and a specialized portion. The general portion includes data and file organization, principles and techniques of programming, interaction with hardware and software, interaction with people, and associated techniques. The programmer then completes the specialized portion in business programming, scientific programming, or systems programming, depending on his or her area of expertise.

To receive either the CDP or the CCP, one must pass the examinations and accept the ICCP Codes of Ethics, Conduct, and Good Practice. In addition, applicants for the CDP must have a minimum of five years' computer work experience. Both examinations are administered by the

Psychological Corporation, a New York-based research and testing organization.

This certification procedure has been in existence for over 25 years, but not without some controversy. The point has been made that although certification sets some minimum standards, it does not necessarily qualify a person to do a job. Having the certificate is a positive accomplishment, but it is not the key to getting hired, even though ICCP is promoting certification both to data processing professionals and to those who hire them. One problem with the test is keeping it up-to-date, as the technology changes rapidly. In addition, if a certificate has not been issued recently, it is based on an examination whose content has become obsolete.

One fact stands out, though: leading individuals in computer careers and professional associations desire to establish the professionalism of their field as has been done in other professions such as law, medicine, and accounting. They are willing to spend time and energy to develop standards of performance and good practice.

To gain more information about the ICCP and the CDP and CCP certificates, write:

> Institute for Certification
> of Computer Professionals
> 2200 E. Devon Ave., Suite 268
> Des Plaines, IL 60018

SOURCES OF ADDITIONAL INFORMATION

Publications

Numerous resources are available to those interested in computer careers, including computer periodicals, journals, and professional organizations. Computer periodicals and journals are excellent sources of general information. They differ in degree of technical depth. Some are written more for information managers and are more applications-oriented, such as *Computer Decisions, Data Management,* and *Infosystems*. Others are written for those in engineering and electronics, such as *Computer Design* and *Solid State Technology*. There are hundreds of periodicals published today in the area of computer technology and its applications. To see this impressive list, one can find *Ulrich's International Periodicals Directory* in the reference section of the library. It is published annually by R. R. Bowker Company, New York and London.

A good many computer periodicals can be found in public and university libraries. The following is a short list of well-known periodicals and the group of computer professionals for whom they are written. Much of the information in this chapter was obtained from these publications.

BYTE	Personal computer users
Computer Decisions	Information processing managers
Computer Design	Designers and engineers
Computer Graphics Today	Computer graphics professionals
Computers and Security	Computer security professionals
Computerworld	Everyone interested in computers
Data Communications	Data communications users
Data Management	Information processing professionals
Datamation	Information processing professionals
IEEE Network	Electrical and electronics engineers
Information Week	Information processing professionals
Information Systems	Information processing professionals
InfoWorld	Personal computer users and suppliers
Journal of Systems and Software	Analysts and programmers
Modern Office Technology	Word processing professionals
Office Telecommunications	Word processing professionals Communications specialists

Organizations

A tremendous amount of current information is disseminated through professional organizations, which encourage students to participate by offering student memberships at greatly reduced rates. The following list of associations provides sources of information in computer fields for both prospective and established computer professionals over a wide range of interest areas:

American Association for
Artificial Intelligence
445 Burgess Drive
Menlo Park, CA 94025

American Federation of
Information Processing
Societies
1899 Preston White Drive
Reston, VA 22091

American Society for
Information Science
1424 16th Street N.W., Suite 404
Washington, DC 20036

Associated Information Managers
3821-F S. George Mason Drive
Falls Church, VA 22041

Association for Computational
Linguistics
Bell Communications Research
445 South Street MRE 2A379
Morristown, NJ 07960

Association for Computer
Educators
College of Business—IDS
James Madison University
Harrisonburg, VA 22807

Association of Computer Users
P.O. Box 2189
Berkeley, CA 94702

Association for Computers
and the Humanities
Humanities Research Center
Brigham Young University
Provo, UT 84602

Association for Computing
Machinery
11 W. 42nd Street
New York, NY 10036

Association for Information
and Image Management
1100 Wayne Avenue, Suite 1100
Silver Spring, MD 20910

Association of Information
Systems Professionals
104 Wilmot Road, Suite 201
Deerfield, IL 60015

Association of Rehabilitation
Programs in Data Processing
P.O. Box 2392
Gaithersburg, MD 20879

Association for Systems
Management
24587 Bagley Road
Cleveland, OH 44138

Association for Women in
Computing
P.O. Box 21100
St. Paul, MN 55123

Common
111 E. Wacker Drive
Chicago, IL 60601

Computer Society of the Institute
of Electrical and Electronics
Engineers
1730 Massachusetts Avenue N.W.
Washington, DC 20036-1903

Data Processing Management
Association
505 Busse Highway
Park Ridge, IL 60068

EDP Auditors Association
455 E. Kehoe Blvd., #106
P.O. Box 88180
Carol Stream, IL 60188

Independent Computer
Consultants Association
P.O. Box 27412
St. Louis, MO 63141

Office Automation Society
International
15269 Mimosa Trail
Dumfries, VA 22026

Society for Computer Simulation
P.O. Box 17900
San Diego, CA 92117

Society for Industrial and
Applied Mathematics
117 S. 17th St.
Philadelphia, PA 19103

Society for Information
Management
111 E. Wacker Drive, Suite 600
Chicago, IL 60601

Society of Telecommunications
Consultants
1841 Broadway, Suite 1203
New York, NY 10023

Telecommunications Industry
Association
1722 I Street, N.W., Suite 300
Washington, DC 20006

Women in Information
Processing
Lock Box 39173
Washington, DC 20016

World Computer Graphics
Association
2033 M Street, Suite 399
Washington, DC 20036

A number of books have been written on computer careers. They provide additional, in-depth information. Check your college library or career information center.

CAREER DECISION-MAKING MODEL

Using the career decision-making model, find out how a career in computers or information processing rates with you. Figure 3-3 is a form with the factors included in the career decision-making model described in detail in Chapter 1. Follow these directions in completing it.

1. Enter the position that interests you most on the line titled *Job*.
2. Enter any additional factors used to personalize your model (from Chapter 1) in the blank spaces provided.
3. Enter the weights that you assigned to the factors (from Chapter 1) in the column *WT*. (It would be wise to review the explanations of the factors in the description of the model in Chapter 1 before going on to step 4.)
4. Assign a value from 1 (lowest) to 10 (highest) to each factor based on the information in this chapter and on your personal self-assessment, entering the value in the column *V*. If you feel that you have a certain aptitude or attribute needed for success in this career area, you should assign a fairly high value. If a certain interest, such as amount of variety, is desirable to you and you feel the area provides the variety you enjoy, assign a fairly high value. If not, assign a low value. Use this technique to assign values to all factors in the model. If you cannot assign a value based on the information in the chapter for some of the factors in the model, either use other sources to acquire the information or leave the space beside the factor blank.
5. Multiply the weight times the value, entering the score in the column *S*.
6. Add the scores in column S for each group of factors entering the number in the space labeled *Total*.

You will use this evaluation in Chapter 11 in combination with evaluations of each career explored in this book.

WHAT DID YOU LEARN?

You learned a lot about careers in computers and information processing in this chapter. Now you should know what these professionals do on the job, where they are employed, what salaries they earn, what kind of job mobility they have, what prevalent trends in the computer industry might affect their jobs, what job opportunities will be in the future, how to pre-

Figure 3-3 Career evaluation for computers

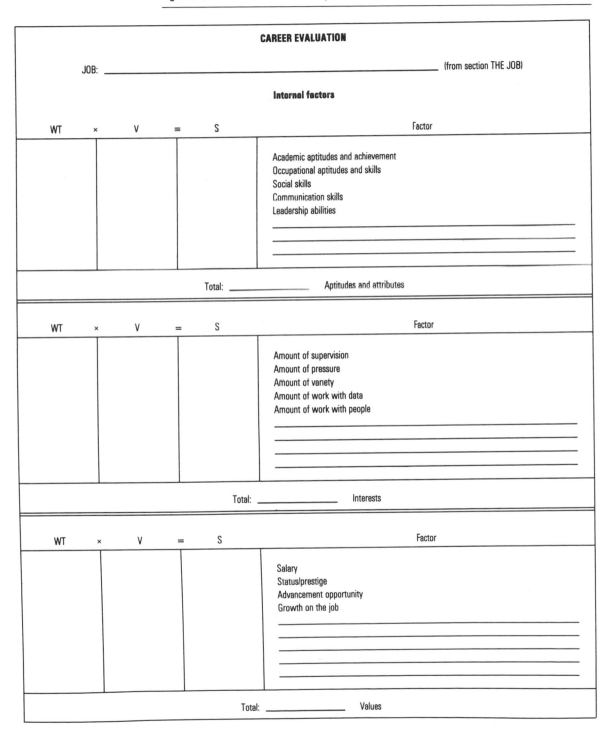

CAREER EVALUATION

JOB: _____ (from section THE JOB)

Internal factors

WT   ×   V   =   S   Factor

Academic aptitudes and achievement
Occupational aptitudes and skills
Social skills
Communication skills
Leadership abilities

Total: _____ Aptitudes and attributes

WT   ×   V   =   S   Factor

Amount of supervision
Amount of pressure
Amount of variety
Amount of work with data
Amount of work with people

Total: _____ Interests

WT   ×   V   =   S   Factor

Salary
Status/prestige
Advancement opportunity
Growth on the job

Total: _____ Values

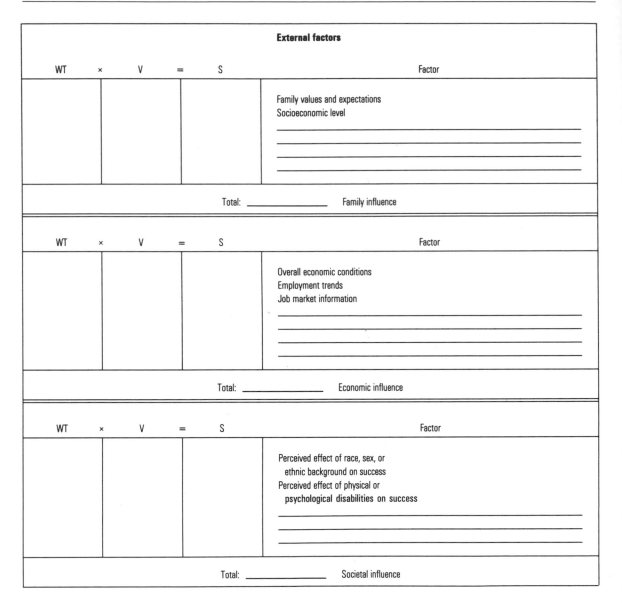

External factors

WT	×	V	=	S	Factor
					Family values and expectations
					Socioeconomic level
					_____
					_____
					_____
					_____

Total: _____   Family influence

WT	×	V	=	S	Factor
					Overall economic conditions
					Employment trends
					Job market information
					_____
					_____
					_____

Total: _____   Economic influence

WT	×	V	=	S	Factor
					Perceived effect of race, sex, or
					ethnic background on success
					Perceived effect of physical or
					psychological disabilities on success
					_____
					_____
					_____

Total: _____   Societal influence

pare for a job in computer and information fields, and where to get additional information. You completed a career evaluation for computers.

Chapter 4, "Careers in Finance," will give you similar types of information about work in the interesting areas of banking, securities, and credit.

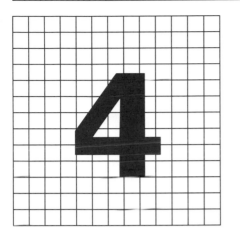

CAREERS IN FINANCE

CHAPTER OBJECTIVES

Upon completion of this chapter, you should be able to:

1. Describe the work of financial specialists in the areas of banking, consumer credit, corporate finance, and securities.
2. Discuss trends in the field of finance and their impact on financial careers.
3. Diagram typical career paths in financial areas.
4. Discuss job opportunities in banking, consumer credit, corporate finance, and securities.
5. List the educational preparation and skills needed to enter financial careers.
6. Evaluate careers in finance according to your individualized career decision-making model.

Finance, the art of administering and managing money, is crucial to the success of every business enterprise. The field of finance has undergone tremendous change over the past decade. A wave of acquisitions, mergers, and divestitures devised by financiers has had much impact on the identities of America's best known corporations. Prompted by government deregulation, the financial field has undergone complex changes both within and between the various financial institutions. The nature of banking has changed as a variety of new financial products has been introduced into the marketplace. The line between commercial and investment banking has disintegrated as both types of institutions now offer similar products, including insurance, while insurance companies now sell securities. Huge financial conglomerates offering every type of financial service—including banking, brokerage, real estate, and insurance—are the way of the future because of the failures, acquisitions, and mergers currently taking place. Changes in the field of finance have many career implications for those entering the ranks.

According to the U.S. Department of Labor's Bureau of Labor Statistics, financial services will grow faster than services as a whole. Financial products such as certificates of deposit (CDs), mutual funds, limited partnerships, bond funds, and variable annuities, as well as life and disability insurance, are especially attractive to middle- and upper-income-level professionals. From parents providing for their children's college expenses to the extremely wealthy, clients flock to estate and financial planners who use sophisticated computer programs to analyze and evaluate financial alternatives. The fastest growth is expected in insurance companies, banks, and credit agencies. Financial services ranks high in average income for finance professionals as well as in career satisfaction.

This chapter will enable you to look at a wide variety of careers in the field of finance. It includes such information as:

- what financial specialists do
- who employs them
- salaries and career paths
- latest trends
- job opportunities
- education and skills needed to pursue a career in finance
- sources of additional information on financial careers

THE JOB

Because of the variety of careers in finance, jobs will be discussed in four major areas: (1) banking, (2) consumer credit, (3) corporate finance, and (4) securities.

Banking

Deregulation has changed the focus of banking. Operational efficiency, the emphasis in the past, has given way to selling the bank's services, which today are many and varied. Competition from other financial institutions such as brokerage firms and insurance companies has posed new challenges for bankers. Banking had been separate from the securities industry for roughly half a century because of the Glass-Steagall Banking Act of 1933, which forbids institutions that take deposits and make loans from doing investment banking. The act also restricts risky banking practices and insures bank deposits by having created the Federal Deposit Insurance Corporation (FDIC). However, the act may be repealed in the immediate future. Meanwhile, the securities industry has begun to offer such products as cash management and ready asset accounts that compete directly with bank products. Banks in turn, as a result of a recent U.S. Supreme Court decision, are now able to underwrite commercial paper, municipal revenue bonds, and other securities.

Large banks hire new college graduates as *bank trainees* to work in specific areas including corporate finance (leveraged buyouts and mergers and acquisitions), sales and trading, retail banking, credit cards, mortgages, branch management, fee-based services, operations and systems, and audit. Trainees are rotated through product and industry specialties within these areas. Managers determine the best permanent place for each individual after completing the training program. Many college graduates "move to the line" after training, which is bank jargon meaning become *bank officers*.

Commercial Loan Officer.   The commercial loan officer is responsible for deciding whether the bank will finance business or corporate ventures. These ventures include such things as the acquisition of another company, new product development, plant expansion, farm production, equipment leasing, short-term loans, and community improvements. Big banks lend to corporations and governments all over the world, including the U.S. government. Commercial loan officers usually specialize further, for example, in local companies or major corporations. The commercial loan officer faces continuous change in the economy, a fast pace, and considerable risk taking. Influence and promotability in the bank are indicated by the size of the loan the officer is authorized to make.

Working closely with the loan officer are the *credit investigators and analysts* who compile the financial data on loan applicants. The loan officer bases a decision of whether to lend the money on these data. Often an employee might begin as a credit investigator or analyst then move into a position as a commercial loan officer.

Consumer Bank Officer.   Working with individual customers on a personal basis is becoming more important as consumer transactions become an increasingly larger chunk of the banking business. The consumer bank officer sells as many of the bank's services as possible to the customer—loans; asset, savings, and checking accounts; certificates of deposit; travelers' checks; and safe deposit boxes, to name the major ones. Within the area of consumer loans, the officer may specialize further, for example, in home mortgages or automobile financing.

Trust Administrator.   The trust administrator has a constructive and humanly rewarding position in the bank. Responsible for helping individuals and corporations manage their financial assets, the trust administrator is knowledgeable in how to use trust techniques to minimize the negative effects of inflation and taxes. Trust administrators may work with a number of different types of financial instruments and trusts, including living trusts, which enable people to better manage their assets while they are alive; Individual Retirement Accounts (IRAs) to shelter income from taxes; various estate planning trusts to plan how their assets will be distributed among their heirs and/or to charities after their death while minimizing taxes; life insurance trusts; corporate pension and profit-sharing funds; trusts holding politicians' assets during their period of government service; and property management for income-producing real estate.

International Banking Officer.   Most large and medium-sized banks have accounts located throughout the world. The international banking officer is responsible for maintaining the balance of these accounts and determining the foreign exchange position. International banking sometimes involves figuring at what price currency can be purchased or sold by reading financial reports and money market quotations. An international banking officer also may sell foreign exchange drafts and determine what proceeds of the sale will go to the bank. Usually a person specializes, dealing with one or two currencies in one part of the world.

Ours has become a global economy as trade barriers are relaxed throughout Europe and the rest of the world. World banking is now common, and international banking expertise will be in much demand in the future.

Bank Manager.   There are numerous levels of managers in big banks. In addition to management positions in all of the areas previously discussed, there are management positions in operations. The operations department is the largest in the bank, largely comprised of clerical employees—tellers, bookkeepers, data entry and computer operators, customer service representatives, and others. A bank manager in the operations department supervises these employees and keeps the bank running smoothly on a day-to-day basis. In today's age of electronic banking, knowledge of computers, telecommunications, and other high-technology equipment is important for managing various facets of operations.

Managerial positions such as *branch bank manager* are open to bank officers with promise. After an executive training program providing experience in a variety of banking activities, an individual may be assigned to a branch bank as branch bank manager. The branch manager usually works under pleasant, fairly autonomous conditions, reporting only to upper-level executives of the main bank. Responsibilities include supervision of branch employees, final decisions on loans, and ideas for new services, procedures, or security to improve the efficiency of the bank. To be effective, the branch manager must be aware of local business, economic, and social conditions.

Moving up the career ladder, bank officers and managers may aspire to such executive levels as *assistant vice-president*, *vice-president*, or even *bank president*. Why not? Promotion from within and conservatism in general in banks suggest that career service pays off.

Opportunities with the Federal Reserve System.   In addition to the positions found throughout the Federal Reserve Banks and their branches, the Federal Reserve System employs *bank examiners* who conduct semiannual, weeklong, on-site examinations, called *internal audits*, of the banks and their branches. Bank examiners travel 100 percent of their working time, with frequent paid trips home.

Operations analysts also are employed by the Fed. They travel 30 percent of the time and assure that such operations as information systems and communications networks are functioning according to established procedures.

Consumer Credit

The rapidly growing career area of consumer credit deserves special attention. Because it is the American way to buy on credit, now more than ever before, credit itself has become a field that is rich in job opportunities.

Most forms of consumer credit fall into one of two types. The first type—noninstallment credit—involves a bill that is paid in one payment. It includes single-payment cash loans, 30-day charge accounts, and such service credit as medical, telephone, and utilities.

The second type of credit—installment credit—involves bills that are paid in two or more installments. Most job opportunities in consumer credit are related to *installment cash credit* and *installment sales credit*. Consumer finance companies extend installment cash credit in the form of cash to consumers to be spent according to their needs. Sales finance companies offer installment sales credit to enable consumers to "buy on time" whatever merchandise or services they need, for example, an automobile or a membership in a health club. A special kind of credit, *mortgage credit*, is used to purchase a home. Consumer finance and sales finance companies compete with banks, savings and loan companies, department stores, and credit unions. Also, large corporations provide credit to consumers as an incentive to purchase their company's goods and services.

Consumer Credit Jobs.   Positions in consumer credit are similar in most institutions. *Consumer credit counselors* interview customers to gather credit information, explain arrangements for making payments, and complete supporting papers. They work with customers to help them decide whether they can afford the credit they are seeking. The decision to extend credit is made by a *credit officer*. Individuals are involved in collections to monitor payments. The *credit manager* may be in charge of a credit department of a store, of a credit union, of the loan department of a savings and loan, of the consumer loan department of a bank, or of a specialized area in a consumer finance or a sales finance company.

Consumer credit, then, is a specialized area of finance careers offering many opportunities for employment and advancement. The field of consumer credit, like all careers in finance, is becoming more sophisticated and complex. For example, students interested in consumer credit today will enroll in such new courses as computer applications to credit; financial decision making; managerial psychology; international credit and finance; and modern marketing strategy keyed to financial and manufacturing policy.

Corporate Finance

Chief Financial Officer.   At the top of the ladder in corporate finance is the chief financial officer, usually titled *vice-president of finance*. This executive is in line for the position of chief executive officer (CEO) of the company. In fact, the largest percentage of the CEOs of major corporations today have risen through the finance or accounting ranks. Responsibilities include participation with other key executives in developing company policy and implementation of financial policy within the organization.

Promotion to this position used to be from within the organization and based on length of service and dedication to the company. This is no longer always true. More companies are hiring professional managers with strong credentials and experience in finance who, rather than moving up in a single corporate hierarchy, have moved laterally from one position of financial management to another, even across industries.

Treasurer and Controller. The key elements of effective financial management are those performed by or supervised by the chief financial officer, the treasurer, and the controller. The *treasurer* has two major responsibilities—the acquisition of funds and the administration and protection of funds. The *controller* manages accounting and other financial information systems, conducts financial planning and performance evaluation, and complies with the requirements of the Internal Revenue Service and other regulatory agencies.

The controller and treasurer may have educational backgrounds in either accounting or finance. Entry-level employees work in either the treasurer's or controller's domain, depending on their background and interest. An individual with a master of business administration degree (an MBA) might be hired as a *financial analyst*. This position was established primarily to speed the entry into a line position in a large corporation. Responsibilities include the analysis of overall financial operations, policies, or problems of the company and the preparation of reports making specific recommendations to management.

Pension Fund Manager. Another opportunity for employment within most large corporations is in the position of pension fund manager. The responsibilities of this position depend on how the fund is managed. The *balanced fund manager* treats the fund as a total portfolio that is actively managed by the corporation itself. The trend today, however, is away from this and toward dividing the fund among *professional money managers* who are usually industry specialists working for money management firms. This reduces the extent of responsibility and status of the pension fund manager, who may find the job to be potentially a dead end.

Positions in Financial Public Relations. An area in corporate finance that is experiencing a demand is financial public relations. Responsibilities associated with a position in financial public relations include financial publicity, stockholder correspondence, stockholder surveys, preparation of annual financial reports or quarterly earnings statements, and financial and educational advertising. Financial public relations personnel also may be involved in planning annual stockholders' meetings and working with security analysts.

Securities

The securities industry involves the buying and selling of stocks, bonds, government issues, shares in mutual funds, or other types of financial instruments. The four basic functional areas are sales, trading, underwriting, and research. Sales and trading personnel must pass the Series 7 section of the National Association of Securities Dealers (NASD) examination to become a registered sales representative. To qualify to take the exam, individuals must be sponsored by a NASD firm. Principals or partners in these firms must pass two exams: Series 7, testing general securities knowledge, and Series 24, testing knowledge of securities rules and regulations. The Series 6 exam is required of mutual fund employees, and Series 52 is required of municipal bond sales representatives.

Sales. Both individual investors and organizations with millions of dollars to invest work through *securities sales representatives*, also called *registered representatives* or *stockbrokers*. These securities sales representatives provide numerous services to their customers, including financial counseling; advice on the purchase or sale of a particular security; development of a financial portfolio including securities, life insurance, and other investments according to the needs of the individual customer; the latest stock and bond quotations on any security that interests the investor; information on activities and the financial positions of companies; and sale of securities for a commission. Securities sales representatives may specialize by customer—for example, small individual investors, large institutional investors, or pension fund managers—and by the type of security—for example, stocks, corporate bonds, municipal bonds, federal government or agency bonds and notes, stock options, commodity futures, mutual funds, or annuities.

Financial Planners. Financial planners work for themselves, alone or in groups. New investment opportunities and confusing tax laws make financial planning an area in great demand today. Financial planners provide services to individuals or to such organizations as banks, corporations, brokerage houses, insurance companies, and savings and loan associations. They also are called *money managers* or *investment counselors*. Clients may be provided with a complete money management strategy—that is, a workable budget, adequate insurance, an investment program, a will, and an estate plan or trust. Financial planners may specialize by industry rather than providing a wide range of services. In this case, they would sell a client on investing a sizable portion of available investment funds in a particular industry. Financial planners may work for large or small financial services firms, banks, or insurance companies, or they may be self-employed.

The designation certified financial planner (CFP) is becoming an industry standard. To achieve this title, one must have completed six specified courses, performed successfully on six exams over a two-year period, worked a minimum of three years in financial planning, signed an ethics statement, and passed a background check.

Trading.   Traders do not deal with individual investors. Rather, they work for an investment firm. *Floor brokers* spend their entire working day on the trading floor at the New York or American stock exchanges, filling their own investment firm's buy-and-sell orders or developing an inventory of particular securities. Traders also may trade securities with other firms. They specialize by type of security, as do *security sales representatives*.

Traders who deal in commodity futures spend their days at the Chicago Board of Trade buying and selling such things as mortgages and soybeans for a given price at a future time, as much as 18 months hence. Traders must have a high level of expertise and be able to make quick judgments.

Underwriting.   Investment banking is carried on by an investment banking firm or a group of investment bankers. Essentially, the *investment banker* underwrites or finances the sale of a corporation's securities to the public by purchasing the securities then selling them on the open market. In recent years, the role has expanded to include structuring joint ventures as well as providing assistance in lease financing, interest rate and currency hedging, and acquisition advising. Investment bankers also may create new financial instruments.

Because of the enormous amount of capital involved, this is one of the riskiest, most challenging, exciting areas of finance. If the stock sells, handsome profits will be made. If it doesn't, the investment banker suffers loss of prestige as well as money. Only top-level professionals are employed as investment bankers, and success is crucial to maintaining their status.

Research.   Securities research and analysis is crucial to the sales, trading, and underwriting of securities. *Securities analysts* provide investment advice for sales reps, brokerage firms, institutions, agencies, and the investment community in general. Most analysts specialize by industry in summarizing statistical data, describing short-term and long-term trends in investment risks, and defining measurable economic influences on various investments.

Two specialty areas other than specialization by industry are money market analysis and technical analysis. *Money market analysts* closely watch the activities of the Federal Reserve System and collect information on the money supply, both in the United States and abroad. *Techni-*

cal analysts work with computers to gain timely information for quick trading.

Other Opportunities in the Securities Industry.   The National Association of Securities Dealers (NASD) is the nonprofit trade organization for the securities industry. Its members function on the floors of exchanges and participate in corporate and public finance. NASD retains a paid staff, with additional volunteers from the brokerage community, who enforce the rules of conduct for the securities industry by examining firms once every three years; by reviewing the backgrounds of the registered representatives; by observing, reporting, and analyzing excessive price changes in securities; and by taking disciplinary action when professional standards are not adhered to strictly. Paid employees of NASD include accountants, lawyers, investigators, and financial analysts.

Also investigating the securities industry is the Securities and Exchange Commission (SEC) of the federal government. Opportunities with the SEC range from investigator trainee through senior investigator. The *senior investigator* trains the entry-level worker, who performs such tasks as examining books and records of registered reps, traders, and investment counselors for possible violations of federal securities laws. The SEC monitors all stock offerings to the public to be sure that corporations and investment bankers are providing full and accurate information to potential investors.

Opportunities for work in *international finance* occur in a number of areas. Through investment banking firms that specialize in international operations, a foreign enterprise or government can issue securities to be sold in the United States or can raise capital in other countries. Some American financial institutions are exclusively international in scope, raising capital only for U.S. firms with overseas operations, or are involved in financing the many multinational corporations. Many graduate programs offer specialization in international finance or international affairs, and numerous banks, corporations, and government agencies provide training in this area. Corporations, banks, and other financial organizations pay premium salaries to MBAs who have specialized in international finance.

Financial journalism is still another area in which researchers and analysts who are trained in finance, economics, and statistics find jobs. Financial journalists write for such statistical publications as *Standard & Poor's* and *Dun & Bradstreet* or for news publications such as *The Wall Street Journal*, *Forbes*, or *Business Week*. Financial journalism is perhaps the only area of financial careers that has a very tight job market. Because of limited opportunities, those who seek positions as financial journalists must plan an aggressive job search and often accept a position with a very low entry salary. However, once a journalist is established, salary becomes comparable to those in the securities industry in general. A person seeking to enter this field should have not only a good background in finance and business, but also strong writing and communication skills. Computer experience helps as well.

CAREER PATHS AND COMPENSATION

Impressive success stories abound in the financial community. Although it is unlikely that a bank clerk or messenger will rise to the position of bank president, advancement still can be rapid for those with desirable attributes and educational background. For example, Howard Marks rose from trainee to vice-president at Citibank in five years. He had majored in accounting and finance at Wharton with master's work in accounting and marketing at the University of Chicago. While completing his master's degree, he became a summer trainee at Citibank. His specialty was trust banking and his advancement especially fast.

A general bank career path chart can be seen in Figure 4-1. Salary figures have been omitted from the chart for two reasons. First of all, the salary range for similar positions is dependent on the size of the bank and varies widely. Second, salaries within each individual bank may vary for the same job title, depending on the amount of lending authority or scope of responsibility of the bank officer. Here are some general salary figures to give you an idea. An officer trainee in a commercial bank with a bachelor's degree may earn from about $16,000 to $30,000 a year in most banks. MBAs' starting salaries range from $27,000 to $50,000 annually. As you can see, starting salaries vary widely, depending on the bank and the area of expertise. Bank officers earn $60,000 and up in annual base pay plus bonuses ranging from 6 to 30 percent. Bonuses and regular incentives are given for meeting and exceeding projected goals. Other bank employee annual salaries are as follows: Bank clerks earn from $8,000 to $18,200; tellers, from $7,800 to $25,000; collectors, from $12,000 to $18,500.

Investment banking salaries vary with area of expertise and level of education. In the area of corporate finance, analysts start at roughly $31,000 and MBAs at $60,000 annually, with bonuses ranging from 25 to 100 percent. Those in research usually hold MBAs and average $35,000 a year to start. Investment bankers specializing in institutional sales and trading earn commissions on the fees paid by client firms. This might average $45,000 a year plus bonuses. In retail sales, professionals earn from $50,000 to $60,000 annually on average. Investment bank managers can earn $125,000 a year with bonuses of 50 to 100 percent. Salaries and job mobility are high among investment bankers. They usually build their careers on experience gained in the trust departments of commercial banks or in brokerage firms. Six-figure salaries and bonuses are common. However, long hours, high risk, and stress come with the job.

Although it is difficult to pinpoint salaries in banking careers, it is even harder to estimate them for other careers in finance. For example, financial planners earn from $30,000 to $200,000 a year, depending on

Figure 4-1 Bank positions and mobility

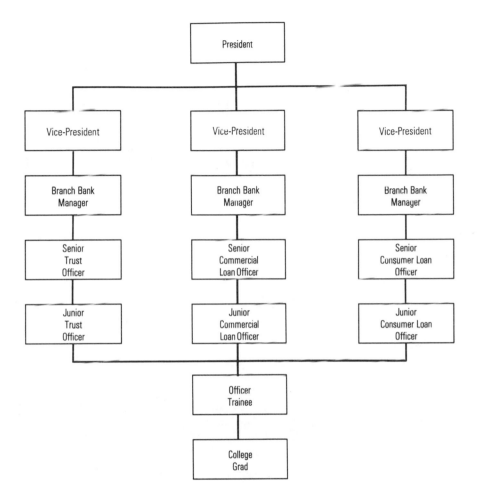

the number and wealth of their clients and their past success. Compensation may be fee only, commission only, or a combination of the two.

Some general career paths for careers in consumer credit, securities, and corporate finance are depicted in Figure 4-2. Salaries vary greatly for these positions, particularly in the securities industry, where personal effectiveness and sales ability determine earnings.

In 1988, the median annual salary for financial managers was $32,800. The range was wide, with salary depending on the size and location of the organization. Executive positions in corporations, such as treasurer, offer expected earnings from $60,000 to $85,000 a year, plus bonuses. Considerable mobility exists between corporate America and the securities industry. If upward mobility in a corporation seems questionable to an individual, brokerage houses and investment firms offer

Figure 4-2 Positions and mobility in consumer credit, securities, firm, and corporate finance

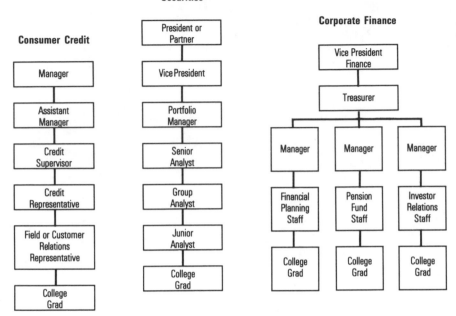

salaries comparable to the treasurer range for well-qualified individuals. On the other hand, Wall Street has its own type of career crisis. Many financial analysts peak early and feel a lack of opportunity for career growth and higher salary. Annual starting salaries for brokers average $15,000 to $25,000. After one year, salaries are supplemented by commissions. Experienced, successful brokers earn up to $175,000 a year. Junior market analysts usually hold MBAs and begin at annual salaries ranging from $18,000 to $22,500. Analysts average from $40,000 to $45,000 in annual salaries. Senior analysts can earn over $100,000, some as much as $300,000, including bonuses. Commodity traders employed by commodity trading companies average from $60,000 to $100,000 annually. Floor brokers can earn from $24,000 to $150,000 a year, and their work is exceptionally stressful.

Remember that it is not unusual any longer for corporations to recruit outside the corporation for key financial executives. An important consideration in any move to a corporation from Wall Street is whether entry into the mainstream or the company's long-range financial planning and acquisition programs is likely. Some analysts have taken a detour that has proved to be somewhat of a dead end into an investor relations position. It is harder to move into a key management position from investor relations. Also, investor relations salaries are substantially less than the salaries successful security analysts get.

As you have seen, industry employment offers salaries that are at least competitive with Wall Street, and mobility between the two is common. But salary isn't everything! In the upcoming section "Aptitudes and Attributes Necded for Success," some contrasts will be made between industry and Wall Street that will enable you to make some judgments about how well you might fit into either world.

CURRENT TRENDS

The financial field is expected to undergo continued changes. The entire financial arena is shifting from national to global markets. Multinational corporations contend with shifting dollar values. Large brokerage firms are participating in foreign exchanges in London, Tokyo, and Sydney. The need now is to have financial analysts who are fluent in foreign languages and understand foreign customs, cultures, and politics.

New technologies permit rapid exchanges of dollars and information. The development of electronic funds transfer and expanded network systems requires financial officers with technical backgrounds. The need for more financial information is creating new information services and blending financial and publishing industries, such as the joint venture between Citibank and McGraw-Hill.

Financial firms have diversified with new products, multiple types of accounts, and investment services. Banks, savings and loans, insurance companies, security dealers, and retailers now provide the same services. Sears has been leading the field of acquisitions and creating its own financial network. The financial field probably will see even greater job mobility.

The growing complexity of the financial field also is increasing the role of financial planner. In 1985, the International Association of Financial Planners grew to 20,000 members, a rate of 30 percent per year. Given the demand and potential to earn large salaries, many unqualified people have entered the market. Future licensing or certification of planners may result.

These are but a few of the trends in the ever-changing finance community. Trends in job opportunities will be discussed in the next section.

JOB OPPORTUNITIES

Demand

Banking is a growth industry, with over 50,000 banking offices in the United States and over 1.3 million workers. The U.S. Department of Labor predicts that the employment of bank officers and managers will increase rapidly through 1995, reaching a total of 530,000. Some advantages that big banks have over small banks are higher salaries and fringe benefits, excellent in-house training programs, a promotion-from-within policy, and rare layoffs of workers even during recessionary times. Some of the recent problems within the banking industry have created a need for more bank examiners to be hired by the Federal Deposit Insurance Corporation (FDIC).

More than 155,000 people currently are employed in the consumer credit industry, and the field is growing rapidly. The Bureau of Labor Statistics projects a 40.9 percent increase in credit analysts by 1995, the seventh-fastest-growing occupation. As in most industries, there are advantages for small companies and advantages in working for large companies. Working for a small company would provide you more opportunity to grasp the overall operation. This is excellent preparation for a position of greater responsibility should the company expand or should you decide to go into business for yourself. Larger companies have a wider range and more levels of positions, therefore offering the possibility of more rapid promotion.

Competition for positions in corporate finance is somewhat greater than for positions in banking and consumer credit. A premium is placed on education. There has been a sharp increase in the demand for personnel in the area of financial public relations.

About 300,000 professionals are employed in the securities industry. Of these, 200,000 are registered representatives. Employment in the securities industry is dependent on the state of Wall Street. Generally, though, the number of securities sales workers will expand as economic growth and rising personal income increase the funds available for investment. A 15.4 percent increase in stockbrokers is expected by 1995. The greatest percentage of change within the financial field is expected in the demand for financial services sales agents. Although the increase is actually only 34,000 new positions by 1995, this represents a 47.8 percent growth.

Equal Opportunity Standing

Although 70 percent of all bank employees are women, the great majority are in low-level clerical and teller jobs. Banking is a conservative, tradition-bound field. Recent successful sex discrimination suits against big banks have helped the advancement of women into management positions. According to the National Association of Bank Women, 40 percent of middle managers are women. Most women managers are locked into lower- and middle-management positions because they lack the educational background or end up in operations, personnel, or branch banks. Most top bank managers come up through the money-making side of banking—the trust department or commercial loans. In the past, big commercial lending was closed to women because of the philosophy that officers must move in elite social circles to solicit new business—private clubs, golf courses, and so on—and that women did not have the same kind of access to these as men. Now some banks have instituted affirmative action programs to give special commercial loan training to female officers. Women officers are increasing in trust departments also as trust services expand. The National Association of Bank Women estimates that only about 13 to 15 percent of all line officer positions are filled by women, but women are moving up.

Only 20 percent of securities sales representatives are women. However, successful women have demonstrated that women can make it in finance. Muriel Siebert, the first woman to buy a seat on the New York Stock Exchange in 1967, when on to become the New York state superintendent of banks. Gloria Markfield was director of money management for Revlon, Inc., at the age of 35, demonstrating that women also can succeed in the corporate financial world.

Members of racial and ethnic minorities are being actively recruited by the banking industry these days. For job referrals, contact:

Bank Administration Institute
60 Gould Center
Rolling Meadows, IL 60008

Board of Governors
Federal Reserve System
Washington, DC 20551

National Association of Bank
  Women, Inc.
500 N. Michigan Avenue
Chicago, IL 60611

Robert Morris Associates
1432 Philadelphia National Bank
  Building
Philadelphia, PA 19107

Minority Applicant Referral
  Service
The American Bankers
  Association
Twentieth Street Station
P.O. Box 19226
Washington, DC 20036

For graduate fellowships in money, banking, and related fields, minority members can write:

Whitney M. Young, Jr., Fellowship
American Bankers Association
1120 Connecticut Avenue N.W.
Washington, DC 20036

APTITUDES AND ATTRIBUTES NEEDED FOR SUCCESS

Education

The best way to tap into the many job opportunities in finance is to get a good education. Although it is claimed that people with a variety of college majors may enter the field of banking, it is probably apparent from what you have learned about mobility that those who successfully move up in bank professions have a solid background in the field of finance. In banking, the best "in" is an educational background in banking, finance, economics, accounting, marketing, or general business. Banks hire people with bachelor's and master's degrees in equal numbers, but an MBA will increase your starting salary by several thousand dollars. In consumer credit, college graduates with business majors in the areas of finance, accounting, economics, statistics, and business law are readily hired. An MBA is good but not necessary. Often the company will finance graduate education.

Although a bachelor's degree in finance, accounting, math, statistics, or economics will gain an entry-level position in the sphere of the treasurer or controller of a corporation, MBAs with technical undergraduate degrees may have an easier time finding employment. A background in computer science or information systems is also advantageous for undergraduates. Opportunities for advancement are good once you get into the mainstream of the corporate financial operation, but competition gets tougher the higher up you go, so it's wise to keep graduate school in mind. Credentials as well as experience will influence progress along your career path in finance.

Personal Characteristics

Educational requirements for entry into the securities industry are about the same as for corporate finance, which in part explains the mobility between them. However, personality characteristics may differ somewhat between Wall Street and corporate professionals. For example, consider the move from a position as a security analyst into a corporation. The brokerage world tolerates the headstrong, independent thinker very well, but in corporations, individuals are more accountable for their actions and must have the cooperative and diplomatic personality required to play the corporate game.

In careers in banking, consumer credit, and the securities industry, human relations and communications skills are very important. For example, in banking and consumer credit such things as a sincere desire to be of service to others, an ability to be friendly but businesslike, tact, and enthusiasm are important. In all finance related fields, such characteristics as personal integrity; precision and accuracy; an ability to analyze facts and make intelligent decisions; an aptitude for math; an ability to work well under pressure; and an ability to handle heavy responsibility are all necessary for success.

Training

Also essential for success in careers in finance is gaining the proper training. Your first job should be carefully selected, with consideration given to the kind of in-house training offered to you by the company as well as the training programs outside the company that will be made available to you through your job. Within the banking industry, consumer credit, and securities industries are institutes, workshops, and training programs for all levels of employees sponsored by industry firms and associations. For example, the New York Institute of Finance is the primary source of training for the securities industry. In banking, courses are offered to member banks by the Bank Administration Institute, the American

Bankers Association, and Robert Morris Associates. Training is stressed by many of the successful people in the field of finance. Certification in those professions where it is available demonstrates commitment to the field and is a big plus in the job market.

SOURCES OF ADDITIONAL INFORMATION

There is a great deal of information available to you if you would like to know more about careers in finance. Such periodicals as *Fortune, Business Week, Forbes, The Banker's Magazine, Banking, American Banking, Trust and Estates, The Money Manager, Financial World, Finance, The Journal of Portfolio Management*, and, of course, *The Wall Street Journal* are just a few of the periodicals from which you can learn a tremendous amount about the field of finance. Listed below are sources to which you may write for information.

For information on banking, write to:

American Bankers Association
1120 Connecticut Avenue N.W.
Washington, DC 20036

Bank Administration Institute
60 Gould Center
Rolling Meadows, IL 60008

For information on consumer credit, write to:

American Financial Services
   Association
1101 14th Street N.W.
Washington, DC 20005

International Consumer Credit
   Association
243 N. Lindbergh Boulevard
St. Louis, Missouri 63141

Credit Union National
   Association, Inc.
5710 Mineral Point Road
Madison, WI 53705

National Association of Credit
   Management
475 Park Avenue South
New York, NY 10015

For information on the securities field, write to:

American Stock Exchange
Information Services Division
86 Trinity Place
New York, NY 10006

Director of Personnel
Securities and Exchange
   Commission
450 Fifth Street N.W.
Washington, DC 20001

Financial Analysts Federation
1633 Broadway
New York, NY 10019

Institute of Certified Financial
   Planners
10065 E. Harvard Avenue, Suite
   320
Denver, CO 80231-5942

Institute of Chartered Financial
   Analysts
P.O. Box 3668
University of Virginia
Charlottesville, VA 22901

International Association for
  Financial Planning, Inc.
Two Concourse Parkway, Suite
  800
Atlanta, GA 30328

Investment Company Institute
1600 M Street N.W., Suite 600
Washington, DC 20036

National Association of Personal
  Financial Advisors
1130 Lake Cook Road, Suite 105
Buffalo Grove, IL 60089

National Association of Securities
  Dealers
1735 K Street N.W.
Washington, DC 20006

New York Stock Exchange
11 Wall Street
New York, NY 10005

Public Securities Association
40 Broad Street, 12th Floor
New York, NY 10004

Securities Industry Association
120 Broadway
New York, NY 10271

Be sure to check your college career information center. You will find many additional sources of information there.

CAREER DECISION-MAKING MODEL

At this point, you should seriously consider the various careers in finance as career possibilities for you. Using the career decision-making model, complete the following form according to the directions. When entering the position that interests you most, try to focus on the *one* area that you would most likely want to work in from among banking, consumer credit, corporate finance, and securities. Figure 4-3 is a form with the factors included in the career decision-making model described in detail in Chapter 1. Follow these directions in completing it.

1. Enter the position that interests you most on the line titled *Job*.
2. Enter any additional factors used to personalize your model (from Chapter 1) in the blank spaces provided.
3. Enter the weights that you assigned to the factors (from Chapter 1) in the column *WT*. (It would be wise to review the explanations of the factors in the description of the model in Chapter 1 before going on to step 4.)
4. Assign a value from 1 (lowest) to 10 (highest) to each factor, based on the information in this chapter and on your personal self-assessment entering the value in the column *V*. If you feel that you have a certain aptitude or attribute needed for success

in this career area, you should assign a fairly high value. If a certain interest, such as amount of variety, is desirable to you and you feel the area provides the variety you enjoy, assign a fairly high value. If not, assign a low value. Use this technique to assign values to all factors in the model. If you cannot assign a value based on the information in the chapter for some of the factors in the model, either use other sources to acquire the information or leave the space beside the factor blank.

5. Multiply the weight times the value entering the score in the column *S*.

6. Add the scores in column S for each group of factors entering the number in the space labeled *Total*.

You will use this evaluation in Chapter 11 in combination with evaluations of each career explored in this book.

WHAT DID YOU LEARN?

You have just learned a great deal about careers in finance. Four areas of possible employment—banking, consumer credit, corporate finance, and securities—were described. Now you know what kind of work finance professionals do, what kinds of salaries they earn, the career paths that many of them follow, what the job outlook is, what trends are affecting it, how to prepare yourself for a marketing career, and where to find additional information. You completed a career evaluation for finance.

In Chapter 5, "Careers in Insurance and Real Estate," you will explore two fields that are among the highest in income potential and add to your knowledge of careers in business.

Figure 4-3. Career evaluation for finance

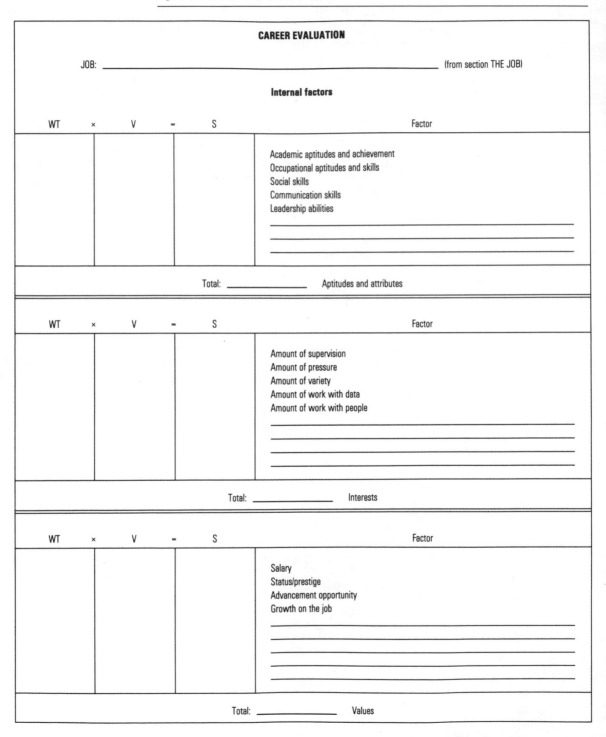

CAREER EVALUATION

JOB: _____ (from section THE JOB)

Internal factors

WT	×	V	=	S	Factor
					Academic aptitudes and achievement
					Occupational aptitudes and skills
					Social skills
					Communication skills
					Leadership abilities

Total: _____ Aptitudes and attributes

WT	×	V	=	S	Factor
					Amount of supervision
					Amount of pressure
					Amount of variety
					Amount of work with data
					Amount of work with people

Total: _____ Interests

WT	×	V	=	S	Factor
					Salary
					Status/prestige
					Advancement opportunity
					Growth on the job

Total: _____ Values

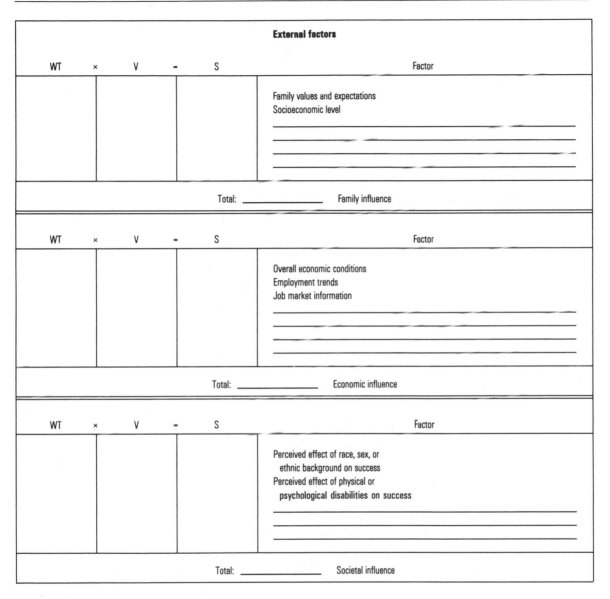

External factors

WT	×	V	-	S	Factor
					Family values and expectations
					Socioeconomic level

Total: _____ Family influence

WT	×	V	-	S	Factor
					Overall economic conditions
					Employment trends
					Job market information

Total: _____ Economic influence

WT	×	V	-	S	Factor
					Perceived effect of race, sex, or
					ethnic background on success
					Perceived effect of physical or
					psychological disabilities on success

Total: _____ Societal influence

CAREERS IN INSURANCE AND REAL ESTATE

CHAPTER OBJECTIVES

Upon completion of this chapter, you should be able to:

1. Describe the work of insurance and real estate professionals.
2. Discuss trends in the insurance and real estate industries and their impact on careers in general.
3. Diagram career paths for professionals in insurance and real estate fields.
4. Discuss job opportunities in insurance and real estate.
5. List the educational preparation and skills needed to enter these fields.
6. Evaluate careers in insurance and real estate according to your individualized career decision-making model.

Buy property and insure it all in once place. Impossible? Not any more. You even can arrange the financing as well. The same changes affecting financial institutions also have influenced the insurance and real estate industries. Government deregulation, expanding technology, and increased financial products have brought these two career fields even closer.

Historically, insurance and real estate have shared common characteristics as career options. First, many people regard opportunities in these areas as sales opportunities. However, both fields offer a variety of career options. In addition to the traditional insurance careers in sales, investments, underwriting, and claims, insurers are becoming involved in a growing number of activities including rehabilitation of injured persons, product safety, industrial hygiene, research, training of commercial drivers, accident prevention, and consumer education. Real estate also is expanding to include real estate appraisal, property management, land development, urban planning, real estate securities and syndication, counseling, research, and mortgage financing.

Second, education and training requirements for insurance and real estate have not been as clear-cut as other areas of business. While on-the-job trainee positions still exist, recent changes require people with more technical knowledge as well as financial backgrounds. To meet the demands, most two- and four-year colleges offer programs. According to the Bureau of Labor Statistics, employment in the areas of insurance, real estate, and finance is expected to grow to 7.8 million by the year 2000.

In addition, both the insurance and real estate fields offer opportunities for autonomy, flexible work schedules, geographic mobility, excellent training, and high income potential.

Careers in insurance and real estate are worthy of consideration because of the variety of positions. This chapter will give you a comprehensive look at both fields. It includes such information as:

- what work insurance and real estate professionals perform
- where they are employed
- salaries and career paths
- latest trends
- job opportunities
- education needed to pursue a career in insurance or real estate
- sources of additional information on insurance and real estate career opportunities

THE JOB: INSURANCE

The insurance industry has two major branches—(1) life and health insurance and (2) property and casualty insurance. Most companies specialize in one of the two. In addition to these is accident and health insurance, which may be written by either type of insurance company. These companies employ individuals in a variety of areas and with a variety of backgrounds. However, the positions described in this section are those unique to the insurance industry itself.

Actuaries.   Insurance premiums are calculated by the amount of risk that a particular policyholder represents. Basically, property-casualty *actuaries* are responsible for analyzing the frequency of catastrophes or chance occurrences such as fires, thefts, sicknesses, and accidents; tabulating the damage they do and the injuries they cause; calculating the mathematical probability or risk associated with recurrences; and then recommending the price or premium that should be charged for insurance against these risks. In the life insurance field, actuaries analyze mortality in order to establish insurance premiums. But that's only part of it! Actuaries in both the property-casualty and life insurance fields play an integral part in determining company policies and practices, assure that the financial reserves of the company are sufficient to pay all claims and expenses, and work with investment analysts to calculate probabilities of loss. To be a successful actuary requires, among other things, an analytical mind and an ability to apply mathematics to practical problems. Once the premiums are established by the actuary, it is up to the agents and brokers to sell policies.

Agents and Brokers.   The work of agents and brokers is selling insurance policies. Insurance sales is basically a three-step process involving *prospecting*, *interviewing*, and *providing service*. Prospecting includes identifying and soliciting potential buyers of insurance. The successful agent will make roughly 40 calls a week and 10 selling interviews to make two sales. Interviewing is conducted to determine the financial needs of individual clients or groups. Services provided by agents and brokers include billing clients, issuing policies, detailed recordkeeping, and response to client questions and needs. This is a crucial aspect of the job since continuing good service leads to more clients.

Agents can work for just one company, or they can operate their own independent agencies, selling insurance for a number of different companies. *Brokers* represent their clients and place insurance policies with the company that offers the best rate and coverage. Often an agent or broker will select a target group such as clients in a certain geographical area, doctors, or college students. Of all life insurance, 42 percent is sold to groups, so group specialists are visable throughout the insurance industry. The *group specialist* works with business firms, unions, or associations rather than with individual policyholders.

Field Representatives.   Providing the liaison between the insurance companies and the insurance agents and brokers who sell the companies' policies are the *field representatives*. These company reps do not sell insurance themselves but rather keep agents and brokers informed of the company's policies and practices and assist them in making sales and servicing customers. The field representative must be poised, diplomatic, and willing to travel, as the position often requires speeches before civic organizations and involvement in public service activities such as fire prevention, traffic control, and safety surveys.

Underwriters.   After a policy has been described and offered for sale by the agent or broker, an application for insurance is made by the client. The job of the *underwriter* is to determine whether the candidate is a good or bad risk. This is done by analyzing information in insurance applications, reports of safety engineers, and actuarial studies. The underwriter in most cases has the final word on whether a policy will be issued. The ability to make personal judgments and the willingness to accept considerable responsibility are essentials of the job. If the underwriter rejects too many risks, the company will lose business to competitors. However, if the underwriter accepts a large number of poor risks, the company may have to pay too many claims.

Underwriters sometimes specialize by the type of risk involved, such as fire, auto, or workers' compensation. Some may handle only business insurance. Usually underwriters work with "packages" which include various types of risks insured under a single policy. No matter how effective an underwriter is in determining which policies are issued, accidents happen and claims are filed.

Claim examiners and adjusters.   Both *claims examiners* and *claims adjusters* are responsible for determining if a loss is covered by the terms of the insurance policy, if the policy is still in force, if the claim is valid, the value of the loss, and the company's obligation. The claims adjuster uses reports, testimony of witnesses, and physical evidence when investigating a claim. The work involves settling valid claims with speed and efficiency while guarding against inflated and false claims. Adjusters may be called to the site of an accident, fire, or burglary at any hour during the day or night. Some adjusters handle several types of claims while others specialize in one area such as auto accident claims and claims of business firms.

Claims examiners work in the home office settling small claims and reviewing the work of the claims adjusters before final settlement with the claimant is made. The work of the claims examiner involves much correspondence, maintenance of records, and preparation of reports to be submitted to the data processing department. Since examiners may be called upon to testify in court on contested claims, they must be thoroughly knowledgeable about their company's settlement procedures and basic policy provisions. Many claims examiners specialize in life, medical, or disability claims

Somewhat related to these private industry positions is the civil service position of *social security claims adjudicator*, who explains to people the government benefits to which they are entitled and how to receive them.

Risk manager.   A loss prevention and insurance specialist usually employed by corporations or firms outside the insurance industry is the *risk manager*. The risk manager is concerned with such risks as property damage, legal liability for faulty products or injuries, fraud, and business interruption. Major responsibilities include estimating the cost of losses in light of these risks, determining the amount of insurance required to cover these losses, and choosing from which company or companies insurance is to be purchased.

The function of the risk manager is highly sophisticated and requires a thorough knowledge of all kinds of insurance as well as a broad business background with emphasis in finance, accounting, and loss control. Risk managers may be involved in employee benefit programs, pension plans, and workers' compensation programs thus working closely with the personnel department. In multinational companies, the risk manager must take on the additional responsibility of educating people overseas in loss prevention and must study how workers of different nationalities might react under conditions of potential danger.

Because of the companywide influence of the risk manager and the required broad educational background, the individual holding this position is an important member of the management team and is involved in major decisions on many complex issues. Most risk managers report directly to a key company executive and may in fact be in line for an executive position.

THE JOB: REAL ESTATE

Real estate has some rather unique advantages over most careers in business. It is one of the few areas in which you can start your own business with a small financial investment and make a great deal of money, or affiliate with someone else without entirely losing your independence and still make a great deal of money. Real estate offers the kind of flexibility that enables individuals to control their own life-styles—you can work part-time or round-the-clock, you can enter a career in real estate at any age, you can earn enough money to retire early or continue to work well past 65, and you can live in any geographical area of the country and change areas without total career disruption.

This section describes the many specialty areas in which people may be employed. *Real estate agents* include both *brokers* and *salespersons.* Brokers, often called *realtors,* are generally in business for themselves, although a few work for large firms where they specialize in managing or selling a particular type of property. Brokers who manage their own firms may be involved in selling, renting, managing, and appraising properties. They must be aware of economic trends, business trends, zoning and other laws, and loans and financing. Brokers employ salespersons who sell and rent real estate for clients and to clients. Selling real estate involves securing property listings, writing descriptive ads, making preliminary appraisals to determine fair market value and to establish price, writing purchase agreements, obtaining seller acceptances, helping buyers arrange financing, and working with title companies or escrow agencies until transactions are completed. In smaller agencies, the broker is involved in selling. In larger agencies, the broker functions entirely in a management position, hiring and training salespersons and managing the office routine.

Residential brokerage.   The largest single field of real estate activity is residential brokerage; that is, helping people buy and sell homes. In smaller communities, most of the homes sold are single-family houses. In urban areas, many clients purchase duplexes, triplexes, and other multifamily dwellings as well as cooperative apartments and condominiums. To succeed as a *residential broker* or salesperson, one must have a broad knowledge of neighborhoods and the people who live there—access to shopping, schools and public transportation, tax and utility rates, building and zoning restrictions, and street and highway plans. An ability to work well with people in gaining an understanding of their tastes, life-styles, and what they are able to afford is essential.

Commercial brokerage.   A *commercial broker* specializes in income-producing properties, such as apartments, office buildings, retail stores, and warehouses. Since commercial property transactions usually involve large sums of money, a commercial broker often may assist the buyer in arranging financing. Successful commercial brokers can understand and explain why properties are good investments in terms of location of property, tax regulations, and advantageous purchasing arrangements.

Industrial Brokerage.   Opportunities are big for the *industrial broker,* who specializes in developing, selling, or leasing properties for industry or manufacturing. Industrial clients will want such information from brokers as availability of transportation, raw materials, water power, and labor supplies; local building, zoning and tax laws; and schools, housing, recreational activities, and cultural facilities for their employees.

Farm and land brokerage.   The *farm broker* needs some agricultural training to estimate the income potential of farmland for prospective buyers. A working knowledge of local soils and the crops best suited for them, planting seasons, water supply, drainage, erosion, farm market centers, transportation facilities, current farm production costs, and latest developments in agricultural technology is essential. Farm brokers also may be involved in farm management for absentee owners. The sale of rural land for urban expansion is another aspect of the farm and land broker's job.

Real estate appraisal.   Although some appraising knowledge is needed for any real estate work, the real pros are the *real estate appraisers.* Appraisers are employed not only by large real estate firms, but also by insurance companies, banks and other lending agencies, government agencies, and tax assessors. The work of the appraiser involves gathering and evaluating all facts affecting the value of a property and rendering an opinion of that value—assessed value for tax purposes, investment value, rental value, insured value, and so on. Appraisers usually have backgrounds in real estate plus mathematics, finance, accounting, and economics and are well-respected in the real estate field.

There is a demand in the marketplace for nonappraisal analyst services to include such areas as site selection studies, competitive property studies, demand studies for space, real estate market studies, environmental impact statements, and land use analyses. Analysis reports are prepared by *real estate analysts* who may also, but not necessarily, be appraisers. Analysts are employed by firms in the design and consulting service industries such as architectural, planning, legal, and real estate counseling firms. Required for entry into this field is a strong background in business, specifically market research, since a major part of the analyst's job is the application of quantitative market research techniques to real estate.

Property management.   *The property manager* is often the key to a successful or unsuccessful investment property. Responsible for supervising every aspect of the property's operation, the manager is involved in renting, rent collection, tenant relations, building and maintenance repair, recordkeeping, and advertising. Property managers usually work for real estate firms but also may find employment in the real estate departments of banks and trust companies or may manage a number of properties for a single owner or corporation. Both commercial and residential properties offer opportunities for professional property managers.

Land development.   Land development is turning raw land into marketable subdivisions, shopping centers, industrial parks, and other residential, commercial, or industrial enterprises. A *land developer* selects sites, analyzes costs, secures financing, contracts for buildings, supervises construction, and promotes the financial development to prospective buyers. To succeed in this profitable, challenging, high-risk area requires business experience and some background in engineering, construction, real estate, and finance.

Urban planning.   The *urban planner* is responsible for proposing productive, economical ways of using land and water resources for urban renewal. Working with local governments and civic groups to anticipate a city's future growth is a critical part of this planning.

Real estate securities and syndication.   A new area increasing in importance is real estate securities and syndication. The *real estate securities and syndication specialist* develops and offers limited partnerships in real estate investments for individuals with limited funds to invest. This service is valuable both to the real estate industry, by generating capital for expanding the industry, and to the individual investor, by providing an opportunity to invest in large properties without becoming involved in the management of them or being exposed to unlimited liability for the investment.

Real estate counseling.   Giving expert advice about property is the work of the *real estate counselor.* Although today very few real estate pros specialize in counseling, this number may increase with the recent heightened interest in real estate investments.

Real estate research.   Trained *real estate researchers* and *economists* are not plentiful because of the extensive technical training in business and economics required to do the job. Research is done in two major areas: (1) physical—that is, how to improve buildings and structures, and (2) economic—that is, compiling data for future planning, such as demand for new homes, changes in financing and interest rates, and the effects of urban planning. Precise information on land use, urban environmental patterns, and market trends is much-needed by business and government, and many employment opportunities exist in real estate research today.

Mortgage financing.   The work of the mortgage financing specialist is to bring together borrowers and lenders. Finding sources of investment money such as insurance companies, banks, savings and loans, and other financial institutions for borrowers is half of the service that mortgage financing specialists provide. The other half is finding good investment properties for lenders and providing them with detailed information about the properties.

A *mortgage broker's* only job is to place the loan; a *mortgage banker* both places and services loans, collecting payments and seeing that taxes and insurance are paid and the property is maintained. Real estate financing specialists find a variety of employment opportunities with both lending institutions and real estate firms.

CAREER PATHS AND COMPENSATION

Some generalizations can be made about the insurance industry relative to salaries. Generally, the larger the company, the higher the salary. Also, specialists in one area of insurance tend to make higher salaries than do generalists. As can be seen in Figure 5-1, the widest salary ranges are at the executive levels and for brokers and agents. Executives employed by large, nationwide companies with tremendous resources, many agents, and vast portfolios of holdings offer top dollar to key executives. Small companies offer much less. Movement from small companies after experience has been acquired is very common. A premium is placed on experience in the insurance industry.

It is difficult to talk about salaries of brokers and agents because they work mostly on a commission basis. Salary is contingent upon the size of the commission, which is determined by such things as the type of insurance, the amount sold, and whether the policy is a new one or a renewal. Beginners often receive a minimum salary or advances on their commissions. Usually agents pay their own expenses, including automobile and travel. For those who own their agencies, expenses such as office rent and clerical wages must be paid. Even so, owners of independent agencies stand to make huge profits if they are successful. Insurance brokers may earn from $25,000 to $100,000 or more depending on the number and type of clients. According to the March 1991 issue of the *College Placement Council Salary Survey*, new bachelor's degree candidates received average annual salary offers of $22,344 in insurance claims and $23,705 in underwriting. For actuarial positions, salaries averaged $30,424 per year.

The insurance industry is a competitive field for beginners, and many who attempt insurance sales eventually leave the field. The agent must have a great deal of initiative and self-confidence to make it. The high

Figure 5-1 Insurance positions, salaries, and mobility

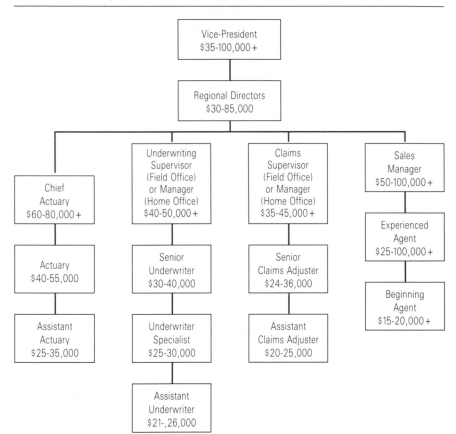

potential of large monetary rewards and the great independence of the job provide the incentives for many to give it a try. The Million Dollar Round Table is a prestigious association honoring members who sell $1 million of life insurance in a year.

Real estate is a unique industry in that titles are relatively unimportant. Status is governed primarily by the amount of sales. Even so, it is often hard to evaluate sales effectiveness since many agents, particularly women, work part time. To give a rough idea—over 500,000 Americans are actively involved in selling residential real estate. Most sell only four or five houses a year. However, a good agent easily can sell $1 million a year in houses and earn an income of $30,000. A really great agent can sell $4 million to $5 million in houses and take home $100,000 or more a year. It is estimated that approximately 10,000 agents and brokers do just that!

Brokers pay salespersons a percentage of the selling price and keep a percentage. A salesperson may earn 7 to 10 percent of the selling price of a property. Therefore, the more inflation drives up housing costs, the more commission agents and brokers earn. Recessions, on the other hand, pose risks to the financial rewards and career development of real estate professionals. When housing starts are down, sales are affected. Although there are some large national real estate firms, the majority of firms in the real estate industry are small local firms that face the risk of going under during recessionary periods.

Real estate appraisers who are tested and certified can earn between $35,000 and $60,000 a year working for private firms and $25,000 a year working for federal agencies. However, their code of ethics prohibits them from accepting any commissions.

Property managers usually are paid a percentage of the rents, typically 10 percent, although they may also receive shares or an interest in the investment. Their careers are built on prior experience in real estate, commercial banking, insurance, or construction.

CURRENT TRENDS

Huge financial conglomerates offering every type of financial service—including banking, brokerage, real estate, and insurance—are the way of the future. Consolidation of services is best exemplified by Sears, Roebuck, Inc. By acquiring the Coldwell Banker real estate firm, Allstate Insurance, and the Dean Witter brokerage house, Sears can provide complete service to clients. Given new packaging schemes, the role of the corporate real estate professional is expanding to include more complex property management functions.

On the other hand, many small, local brokers are affiliating with franchise firms and large corporate structures because they feel a need for national identification. There are about 30 real estate franchise chains growing at a rate of 30 percent annually. National identity is increasingly more important because of the fast-growing number of Americans who move between cities each year. This movement has given birth to a new industry—the relocation business. Totaling as much as $125 million, the relocation industry uses a network of affiliated brokers who buy and sell homes for transferred employees. The brokers pay a fee to the relocation firm, usually 25 percent of the commission.

As for technology, the real estate industry is seeing emergence of the "smart" building and new marketing techniques. John Naisbitt reports on the multitenant megastructures offering computerized operating and monitoring systems, shared telecommunications systems, and sophisticated environments designed to maximize productivity and comfort. Video marketing via telecommunications systems allow clients to view properties without traveling.

Technology has changed the insurance agent's marketing strategies as well. Agents use portable computers instead of rate books to analyze actuarial data, provide instant illustrations, and produce printed output.

Computers have permitted the agent to be even more detached from the office.

Throughout the insurance industry, changes in both the type and the number of product offerings can be seen. The increase in the number of older Americans is creating a demand for more home care plans, retirement home options, and cooperative arrangements between government and insurance companies. Another factor affecting the offerings in the life and health area is rising health costs at a time when AIDS and cancer cases are increasing. In the property/casualty area, new insurance policies are being written to protect against skyjacking, inept securities brokers, and other areas not clearly covered by traditional policies. To compete in the financial services market, insurance companies are offering more tax-deferred products, such as single-premium life insurance policies, and more services, such as financial counseling, estate planning, securities sales, and cash management accounts. With this diversification of products and services come many new job opportunities.

JOB OPPORTUNITIES

The insurance industry employs over 2.2 million people in more than 6,000 companies. Insurance premiums total over $350 billion per year. In general, the insurance industry is relatively stable, fairly immune to the ups and downs of the economic cycle. Most people regard insurance as a necessity. Growth through the year 2000 generally will be at an average rate.

The greatest demand in the insurance industry is for actuaries. Today it is estimated that companies could use two to three times the number of actuaries currently employed. The Bureau of Labor statistics predicts the number of actuaries to double by the year 2000. The most rapidly growing demand for actuaries is in group insurance, particularly pensions. Despite the slowdown in hiring, the industry will continue to expand. The commercial lines of insurance are healthy and there will be a 29 percent increase in the demand for commercial underwriters. The number of insurance sales agents is expected to increase 14 percent by the year 2000. One-third of all insurance employees work in sales. The demand for insurance sales workers, though average, will not keep pace with rising insurance sales due to increased productivity in sales and changing business practices. An increase of 58,000 jobs is expected from 1988 to the year 2000. Opportunities will be best for people who have expertise in a variety of insurance and financial products. Insurance selling is highly competitive and will remain so. Beginners who cannot establish good clients must often leave the field. Only 13 percent of the agents in large life insurance companies last four years.

Unlike the insurance industry, the real estate industry is inextricably linked to the U.S. economy, which runs in cycles from peak to weak periods. A growing volume of sales of residential and commercial properties suggests average growth in real estate positions through the year 2000. For property and real estate managers, an increase of 43,000 jobs—a 19-percent increase—is predicted.

An anticipated increase in the volume of residential and commercial properties will provide average growth in job opportunities for real estate agents, brokers, and appraisers. Though jobs will be available, the best-trained and most ambitious workers are the ones who will survive in this competitive sales environment.

A recent article, "Where the New Jobs Will Be," appearing in the March 1991 issue of *Money* magazine reported the results of a survey. New jobs for underwriters will be available in greatest numbers in the following metropolitan areas over the next five years: Dallas/Fort Worth, Atlanta, Tampa/St. Petersburg, Philadelphia, San Jose, Orlando, San Diego, Denver, Baltimore, Seattle, Essex County (New Jersey), Nashville, Salt Lake City, Indianapolis, and Richmond. Real estate managers will find most new job opportunities in Anaheim, Dallas/Fort Worth, Chicago, Nassau County (New York), Tampa/St. Petersburg, San Diego, Boston, Sacramento, Seattle, Pittsburgh, San Antonio, Greensboro, St. Louis, and Hartford.

Like the insurance industry, there is high turnover and failure among beginning salespeople. Generally, women and minorities have been widely involved in the real estate industry. Various industry studies have shown that neither sex, age, nor race have any bearing on job performance.

Some attributes and backgrounds that do have an effect on job performance in both insurance and real estate are explored in the following section.

APTITUDES AND ATTRIBUTES NEEDED FOR SUCCESS

Insurance

Education. Although a college degree is not strictly required for employment in most careers in insurance, it is preferred by many companies and is essential for promotion to positions of greater responsibility. Over 75 colleges and universities offer undergraduate degree programs in insurance. Actuaries usually have a math or statistics major with some business background and writing skills. A few colleges offer programs in actuarial science. Claims adjusters, underwriters, brokers, and agents usually have bachelor's degrees in business administration and preferably majors in insurance. Courses in economics, accounting, and business law are helpful. Depending on the type of insurance company for which you work, additional preparation might include knowledge of auto repair, medical knowledge, and so on. In commercial insurance, underwriters are almost always expected to have some business experience.

Risk management is an area not to overlook when examining insurance careers. Many universities offer a risk management major or concentration at undergraduate and sometimes at graduate levels. Many organizations offer internships to risk management students both inside and outside the insurance industry. A student might land an internship with a major corporation, a group of risk management consultants, the government, or an insurance company, all of which are promising employers after graduation. Internships last from two weeks to three months, usually during summer vacation. Involved students gain valuable real-world experience and earn money.

Licensing.   Claims adjusters must be licensed in a majority of states, and all agents and most brokers must be state-licensed. Most states require applicants for licenses to pass written exams on insurance fundamentals and state insurance laws. Successful claims adjusters and agents must like dealing with people, must be outgoing, must enjoy travel and variety, and must be well-organized and independent.

Training.   Many insurance companies will pay all or part of tuition costs for additional education. Most large companies have excellent on-the-job training programs. Training might include rotation among various departments enabling new employees to get an overall look at the company and to choose an area in which to work. It is very important to determine what educational and training opportunities a company offers before accepting employment.

Testing.   There are a couple of aptitude tests used throughout the insurance industry. If you are considering an actuarial career, you might want to take the Actuarial Aptitude Test. Inquire about it at your college counseling center or write:

> Society of Actuaries
> 475 N. Martingale Road
> Schaumburg, IL 60173-2226

The Aptitude Index Battery (AIB) is widely used throughout the insurance industry. The Inventory of Insurance Selling Potential also is used in the selection of agents. For information about these two instruments, write:

> Life Insurance Marketing and Research Association
> 170 Sigourney Street
> Hartford, CT 06105

Real Estate

Education and licensing.   Both two- and four-year colleges usually offer courses in real estate. In addition, some background in finance, economics, and psychology is good preparation for a career in real estate.

Many firms and real estate boards offer formal training for salespersons and brokers as preparation for obtaining a state license. Licensing requirements vary from state to state, but all states require prospective salespeople and brokers to pass written exams covering the fundamentals of real estate transactions and state laws affecting the sale of real estate. The real estate boards located in the state capitals can provide you with licensing information for the particular state in which you choose to work.

Among real estate professionals, the majority have had some college education; many have bachelor's degrees. This is not usually a requirement; however, some states such as Texas are moving toward requiring that applicants for a real estate license hold a bachelor's degree. If you are interested in a real estate career, it would be wise to check the state requirements by writing the real estate board before planning your education.

Personal attributes.   Many studies have been conducted to attempt to pinpoint the attributes needed for success. Findings show that successful real estate pros are:

- better able to work alone
- emotionally stable
- tolerant of stress
- full of drive and energy
- trusting of people
- persuasive
- friendly and warm
- results-oriented
- organized
- objective

SOURCES OF ADDITIONAL INFORMATION

There are numerous sources to which you can write for additional information on careers in insurance and real estate. Some of these sources are listed. For information on careers in insurance, write the following:

American Society of CLU and
  CHFC
270 Bryn Mawr Avenue
Bryn Mawr, PA 19010

Association for Advanced Life
  Underwriting
1922 F Street N.W.
Washington, DC 20006

Casualty Actuarial Society
One Penn Plaza
250 W. 34th Street, 51st Floor
New York, NY 10019

Independent Insurance Agents of
  America
127 Peyton
Alexandria, VA 22314

*Insurance Information Institute
110 William Street
New York, NY 10038

Life Insurance Marketing and
  Research Association
Box 208
Hartford, CT 06141

Million Dollar Round Table
325 W. Touhy
Park Ridge, IL 60068

National Association of
  Independent Insurers
Public Relations Department
2600 River Road
Des Plaines, IL 60018

*National Association of
  Insurance Women
1847 East 15th Street
Box 4410
Tulsa, OK 74159

National Association of Life
  Underwriters
1922 F Street N.W.
Washington, DC 20006

Society of Actuaries
475 N. Martingale Road
Schaumburg, IL 60173-2226

Society of Chartered Property
  and Casualty Underwriters
Kahler Hall
720 Providence Road, CB #9
Malvern, PA 19355

The sources with an asterisk can provide you with a list of schools offering undergraduate majors in insurance. You might also write to The College of Insurance. The college is fully accredited, offering BS degrees in actuarial science and in business administration with an insurance major. It is supported by the insurance industry.

The College of Insurance
101 Murray Street
New York, NY 10007

For information on real estate careers plus a list of universities, colleges, and junior colleges offering courses in real estate on campus; a list of state universities offering correspondence courses in real estate; and a list of names and addresses of real estate licensing officials in each state, write to:

National Association of Real
  Estate Brokers
1629 K Street N.W., No. 2
Suite 605
Washington, DC 20006

National Association of Realtors
430 N. Michigan Avenue
Chicago, IL 60611-4087

CAREER DECISION-MAKING MODEL

It is now time to consider a career in insurance or real estate as a possible career for you. Figure 5-2 is a form with the factors included in the career decision-making model described in detail in Chapter 1. Follow these directions in completing it.

1. Enter the position that interests you most on the line titled *Job*.

2. Enter any additional factors used to personalize your model from Chapter 1 in the blank spaces provided.

3. Enter the weights that you assigned to the factors (from Chapter 1) in the column *WT*. (It would be wise to review the explanations of the factors in the description of the model in Chapter 1 before going on to step 4.)

4. Assign a value from 1 (lowest) to 10 (highest) to each factor based on the information in this chapter and on your personal self-assessment entering the value in the column *V*. If you feel that you have a certain aptitude or attribute needed for success in this career area, you should assign a fairly high value. If a certain interest, such as amount of variety, is desirable to you and you feel the area provides the variety you enjoy, assign a fairly high value. If not, assign a low value. Use this technique to assign values to all factors in the model. If you cannot assign a value based on the information in the chapter for some of the factors in the model, either use other sources to acquire the information or leave the space beside the factor blank.

5. Multiply the weight times the value, entering the score in the column *S*.

6. Add the scores in column S for each group of factors entering the number in the space labeled *Total*.

You will use this evaluation in Chapter 11 in combination with evaluations of each career explored in this book.

WHAT DID YOU LEARN?

This chapter described various careers in insurance and real estate. It included information about the nature of the work, areas of specialization, salaries, career paths, current trends, job opportunities, education and attributes needed for success, and sources of additional information. You completed a career evaluation model for insurance and real estate. Chapter 6, "Careers in Marketing," will introduce you to such popular careers as advertising, sales, market research, retailing, and public relations.

Figure 5-2 Career evaluation for insurance and real estate

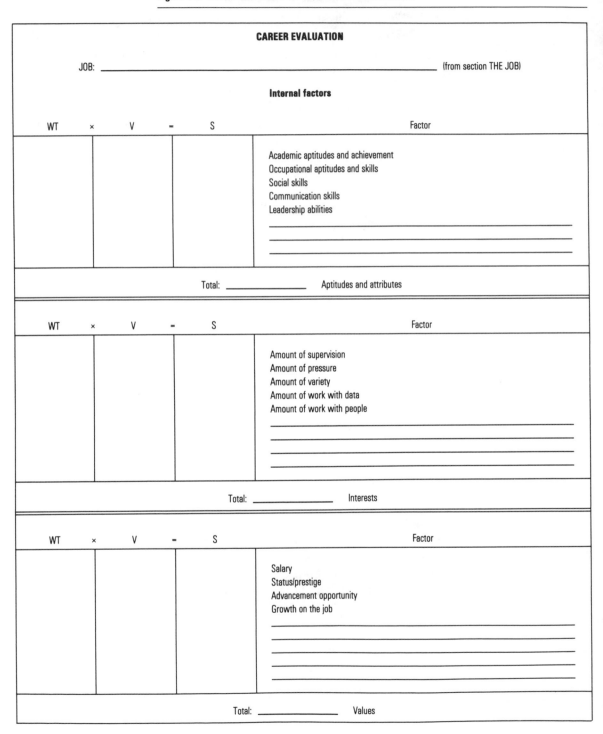

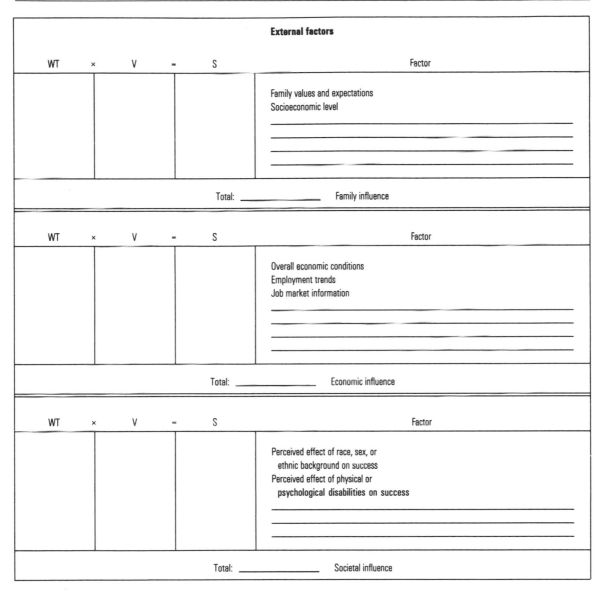

External factors

WT	×	V	=	S	Factor
					Family values and expectations
					Socioeconomic level

Total: _____ Family influence

WT	×	V	=	S	Factor
					Overall economic conditions
					Employment trends
					Job market information

Total: _____ Economic influence

WT	×	V	=	S	Factor
					Perceived effect of race, sex, or
					ethnic background on success
					Perceived effect of physical or
					psychological disabilities on success

Total: _____ Societal influence

CAREERS IN MARKETING

CHAPTER OBJECTIVES

Upon completion of this chapter, you should be able to:

1. Describe the work of marketing professionals in the areas of marketing research; product development; advertising; sales promotion; public relations; wholesale, industrial, retail, and direct selling; and international marketing.

2. Discuss trends in marketing and their impact on the careers in general.

3. Diagram career paths in the field of marketing.

4. Discuss job opportunities in marketing careers.

5. List the educational preparation and skills needed to enter each of the marketing career areas.

6. Evaluate careers in marketing according to your individualized career decision-making model.

Marketing has moved from the peddler who would visit rural settlements annually to complex telemarketing systems that provide at-home shopping to consumers. The board of directors of the American Marketing Association defines marketing as "the process of planning and executing the conception, pricing, promotion, and distribution of ideas, goods, and services to create exchanges that satisfy individual and organizational objectives." The notion of a product has been expanded to include ideas and services as well as goods. As the definition suggests, marketing professionals are involved from the conception of a product that might sell to the actual sale and distribution of a product to the ultimate consumer.

Today, the primary emphasis of marketing is no longer on selling already-planned and produced goods, but rather identifying customer wants and planning products to satisfy these wants. The "marketing concept" is basically a philosophy that focuses on customer wants and identified markets. Companies have found that they can create the desire in potential customers for certain types of products, thus marketing has grown into a complex and sophisticated field needing a large number of highly trained professionals to perform its many specialized functions.

The many facets of marketing are interesting to consider, along with the many career opportunities they provide, such as marketing research, product management, advertising, sales promotion, wholesale and industrial sales, retailing, international marketing, and public relations. This chapter includes such information as:

- what marketing pros do on the job
- who employs them
- salaries and career paths
- latest trends

- job opportunities
- education and skills needed to pursue a career in marketing
- sources of additional information on marketing careers

THE JOB

Marketing is an incredibly broad field involved with a product or service from the time it is conceived until after it is sold, including service and maintenance. Professionals are employed in such fields as advertising, selling, marketing research, product development, promotion, and public relations. Industrial, wholesale, retail, and direct selling provide different channels of distribution for moving products into the marketplace and offer numerous job opportunities. The growth in international marketing has opened new possibilities for marketing professionals.

The demand and variety in marketing careers suggest that as a field, marketing has much to offer. An investigation of careers in marketing will point out not only specific areas of opportunity, such as those outlined above, but also the broader nature of marketing as a whole. Within marketing careers are numerous opportunities for growth and change. Marketing itself is so diverse that most individuals with the resources to attend college can find jobs well-suited to both their skills and interests. Our investigation of marketing careers begins at the start of the marketing process with marketing research.

Marketing Research   Marketing researchers are the pioneers of marketing—exploring new possibilities which sometimes result in revolutionary products that make life easier or more enjoyable. Marketing research begins with the identification of a needed product, which can be a good or a service, by a particular market. Specialists in the area of marketing research identify potential consumer groups, describe them in detail, find out what these consumers want, detail these wants in terms of specific products, determine if such products exist and what competing companies are supplying them, forecast what products consumers are likely to want in the future, and predict which competitors also are likely to produce these products. And that's only part of it!

The marketing research department of a company includes the *marketing research director, research analysts,* and trainees, who hold the position of *junior marketing research analyst.* In addition, a *field service director* hires and supervises *interviewers* and *coders.* Marketing research professionals engage in such activities as identifying market trends, developing customer profiles, monitoring competition, measuring market share, evaluating brand images, designing products and packages, planning distribution channels, assisting in advertising and promotion campaigns, analyzing audience characteristics, and evaluating the impact of advertising and promotion. These individuals generally have degrees in marketing with strong backgrounds in statistics and psychology. *Marketing researchers* are employed by manufacturers of both goods and services, by nonprofit organizations, by marketing research firms, or as independent consultants. Marketing research is not limited to consumer products, but is also conducted in such areas as environmental concerns, business decisions, political campaigns, association images, and a wide range of others.

Recent college graduates are hired as junior or associate analysts who are usually assigned such responsibilities as editing questionnaires, handling correspondence, and collecting data from libraries, company files, or trade journals.

Field service directors, who may have been promoted from junior analysts, hire and supervise field service and tabulation personnel who conduct interviews, enter numbers into the computer, or run standard types of programs. Sometimes the field service director contracts with outside field service firms to perform these activities. Field service and tabulation personnel do not need college degrees, often work for minimum wages, and do not normally advance to other positions in marketing research. The director of field service, however, is an integral member of the marketing research team.

Experienced analysts develop proposals for research projects, develop questionnaires, analyze data, organize studies, and write reports. Advancement to the position of senior analyst and ultimately to the position of research director or head of the marketing research department involves a marketing professional in more and more administrative and supervisory tasks, such as preparing budgets, overseeing projects, and reporting to higher-level marketing management. In marketing research firms, senior analysts also are involved in obtaining new clients.

Product Management

Hundreds of millions of dollars are spent each year to develop and market new products—and roughly 80 percent of these products fail. Insufficient or inaccurate answers to the following questions may cause this.

- Should the product be made?
- Who is expected to buy it?
- What characteristics do consumers want in this type of product?
- What are consumers willing to pay for such a product?
- What competing products are already on the market?
- How is the proposed product better than the existing one(s)?
- What are the best ways to distribute the product?
- How should the product be promoted?

Using information compiled by marketing researchers, companies decide whether to introduce new products into the marketplace. Once a firm makes a commitment to develop a specific product, a *product manager* is assigned or hired to spearhead the project. This position is often entitled *brand manager* in firms that make consumer products. Product managers may be assigned to a product for the duration—from its initial development throughout the length of its life cycle. Sometime, however, *new-product development managers* are assigned for a product's initial development and test marketing, then a product manager is assigned who will take over and remain in charge of the product throughout its life cycle. Special *product recall managers* sometimes are assigned when products posing threats to consumers must be withdrawn from the market.

Normally, the product manager assembles a development team whose members work first with marketing research to further define the characteristics of the product, next with engineers in the design and production phases of product development, then with advertising and sales promotion professionals, and finally with the sales force. Members of the product development team are involved in naming, packaging, and distributing the product. They usually come from different departments throughout the organization. As team members, they are in a unique position to interact with almost every department in the company. Product development can be an excellent avenue of advancement to other positions within the company once a project is completed.

The general responsibilities of product managers, assistant product managers, and their teams are to:

1. Evaluate product testing and recommend whether to terminate development, modify the product, or begin the campaign.
2. Plan the introduction and scheduling of the final product and packaging with the production department.
3. Provide information and recommendations on the price for the product.
4. Develop sales and profitability forecasts and marketing budgets with the finance department.
5. Analyze statistics and recommendations from marketing research to allocate funding for advertising and promotion campaigns.
6. Identify channels of distribution, that is, wholesalers, retailers, and/or direct selling.
7. Work with marketing research and advertising departments to create a favorable image for the product in the minds of consumers.
8. Coordinate the production and promotion of the product.
9. Monitor and evaluate consumer reaction to the product.

Product management is very much like running a small business. Most companies look for entrepreneurial types with a broad knowledge of business. Larger manufacturers hire only MBAs for the entry-level position in product management—assistant product manager. Smaller manufacturers consider candidates with an outstanding undergraduate degree. Advancement may be to the position of product manager. Some companies offering dozens of brands in various categories promote exceptional product managers to the position of *category manager.* Advancement to middle and top-level marketing management is possible from product and category management positions.

Advertising

Of all marketing careers, advertising is perhaps the most competitive area for entry-level positions and advancement. Whether employed by a company or an advertising agency, professionals must work in a highly charged atmosphere with extreme pressure to produce.

In a company, the *advertising manager* determines how the advertising budget will be spent. Advertising professionals may be employed in creative positions in which they design and produce the advertisements. Under the *art director, copywriters* and *artists* help to develop and refine concepts and ad campaigns. The artists provide the visual effect and the copywriters add the words for newspaper, magazine, radio, television, and numerous other advertisements. The *traffic manager* keeps all advertising activities on schedule. These ads are then turned over to *media planners*, who develop marketing strategy, buying air time on television or radio and space in printed media. *Research analysts* perform similar functions to those described in the section on marketing research. They study consumers' perceptions of products and the company's advertising effectiveness, interacting with creative and media personnel both in the production of ads and in the modification of ad campaigns. Corporate advertising managers must decide, for each product, whether to conduct the ad campaign completely in-house or whether to hire an advertising agency for certain ad campaigns.

Advertising professionals employed by agencies perform the same functions as described for a company. Normally advertising agencies have four departments: creative, media, research, and account services. Jobs are equally divided between *account support professionals* (the "suits")—in areas including account services, marketing research, and media planning—and *creative functions professionals* (the "creatives"). In the account services department, an *account executive* plans and oversees the ad campaign and serves as the liaison between the agency and the client. Advancement into account services comes with experience and success in one of the other departments. From the position of account executive, individuals may advance into such positions as *senior account executive, accounts supervisor*, and *accounts manager*.

Sales Promotion

Closely linked to advertising, sales promotion is geared toward individual consumers rather than masses. Advertising suggests while sales promotion motivates. Sales promotion falls into three categories:

1. *Consumer promotion*, including samples, coupons, rebates, games, and contests.
2. *Trade promotion* for intermediaries, including cooperative ads, free goods, and dealer sales contests.
3. *Sales-force promotion*, including such incentives as sales meetings, contests for prizes, and bonuses.

Specialists in sales promotion have previous sales or advertising experience. These professionals may be employed by companies or by sales promotion firms, which play a role similar to advertising agencies.

Sales promotion specialists plan promotional campaigns for products, working with information from marketing research, a product concept, and a specified budget. They direct a creative team, including *artists* and *copywriters*, in designing items such as coupons, free goods, and packages to accomplish the campaign objectives. Coming up with promotion ideas such as contests, games, and rebates also is part of the job. Normally, sales promotion campaigns accompany the introduction of new or improved products, while advertising is ongoing. Sales promotion specialists must have research abilities, administrative skills, and creativity to function well in their positions.

Public Relations

Both sales promotion and advertising focus on a product. The sale of all products in a company may be improved through the creation of goodwill. This is done through the public relations (PR) department, whose objective is to build and maintain a positive image of the company in the eyes of the public. Large companies have a public relations department with a staff of specialists who work under a *director of public relations*. Smaller companies may hire one individual to conduct public relations activities. Some companies contract out work with PR firms that function in the same manner as advertising agencies or sales promotion houses.

Public relations professionals, sometimes called *public relations officers* or *PR reps*, must provide information about the organization to various groups, including government agencies, environmentalists, consumerists, stockholders, and the public at large. This is sometimes done through the creation of publicity, which is free coverage of company activities and philosophy by the media. The entry-level work of public relations professionals usually includes acquiring information from a variety of sources and maintaining files. With experience, PR professionals begin to write press releases, executives' speeches, and articles for both internal and external publications. Other duties include working with media contacts, arranging speaking engagements for company officials, planning special events, and making travel arrangements for prominent people. In PR agencies, individuals begin as assistants and advance to positions as account executives. In this capacity, they work with clients to plan a public relations campaign strategy and see that it is executed.

Public relations professionals are employed by businesses, nonprofit organizations, trade associations, government agencies, colleges, prominent individuals, large advertising agencies with PR departments, and public relations firms that serve a wide range of clients. Individuals need not have marketing degrees to enter public relations and tend to come from an incredibly wide variety of backgrounds. However, they are involved in selling—selling organizations or individuals to the public. Therefore, public relations easily fits into the range of marketing careers. Although the marketing concept is the philosophy of business management, it has been effectively employed by nonbusiness groups such as charities, the arts, educational institutions, federal and local governments, and others. Whether an organization is soliciting funds or promoting ideas, it functions in much the same way as a business selling goods or services.

Sales

Through the efforts of professionals in advertising, sales promotion, and public relations, consumers are made aware of a company's products. The producer must then choose how to move the product from the warehouse to these consumers. This process, called *distribution*, may be done through various channels. Options include the sale of the product to wholesalers, retailers, or directly to the consumer.

Sales and customer service are the keys to running a successful business in today's economy. Professional salespeople are the backbone of any company. Without an effective sales force, a company could not survive in a competitive environment. With so many similar products, it is the sales force that makes the difference. Many marketing graduates start in sales. Sales is a perfect area for beginners truly to learn their company's business and to show what they can do. It is an opportunity where hard work really does pay off, both in increased earnings and in recognition. *Retail sales representatives* offer products to the final consumers in stores of all sizes. *Wholesale or industrial sales representatives* sell both finished products and materials to retailers, other intermediaries, and manufacturers. *Industrial sales representatives* are company-employed by manufacturers. However, they are not the only ones selling the company's products. *Manufacturers' representatives* are independent businesspeople who may sell one or more companies' products to many different customers. Also self-employed are *wholesale dealers*, who find needed products for client companies.

Sales representatives of all types perform numerous activities, including some of the following:

1. Setting goals, planning, and making schedules.
2. Identifying and contacting prospective clients or customers.
3. Maintaining contacts with current customers and anticipating their needs.

4. Planning and making sales presentations.
5. Reviewing sales orders, scheduling delivery dates, and handling special details.
6. Maintaining up-to-date records and reports.
7. Handling complaints and problems.
8. Monitoring the competition.
9. Learning new product information and marketing strategies.
10. Evaluating price trends and advising customers.

Time management is crucial to successful selling. Sales reps must allocate their time carefully among the above activities. High-tech items such as laptop computers, cellular phones, and fax machines enable sales reps to be more efficient. Organization, initiative, and communications skills are vital to successful selling.

Retailing

Retailing is a combination of activities involved in selling goods and services directly to consumers for personal or household use. Retail sales differs from wholesale and industrial sales in that the customer usually comes to the salesperson. Roughly one out of seven full-time workers is employed in retailing. Thousands more hold part-time jobs. Retail professions fall basically into two groups: (1) those involved in merchandising—that is, purchasing the goods offered for sale, including *merchandise managers*, *buyers*, and *assistant buyers*, and (2) those involved in selling goods to the public, including department, regional, and national *sales managers* and *sales representatives*.

Recent college graduates often enter merchandising as assistant buyers. They work under buyers in speaking with manufacturers, placing orders for merchandise, inspecting new merchandise, supervising the distribution of merchandise, and managing inventory. Experienced buyers work under merchandise managers in analyzing customer needs and choosing products to meet them. Merchandise managers supervise buying activities, allocate budgets, and perform primarily administrative tasks. They work closely with department managers who supervise selling activities.

Sales management trainees are recruited from sales positions or from the pool of recent college graduates. These trainees assist the manager in staff scheduling, recordkeeping, and handling customer complaints. The largest number of opportunities in retailing is in sales, with service sales positions creating the most new opportunities. Retail sales representatives, like their industrial and wholesale counterparts, must have good communication skills, an understanding of their customers' needs, knowledge of the competition in some cases, and a positive attitude. Sales is hard but rewarding work for those with the temperament and initiative to do it well.

Direct Marketing

Direct marketing, or nonstore selling, is growing at a faster rate than in-store selling. Every imaginable type of product is sold through direct marketing today—apparel, books, plants, high-tech items, portraits, insurance, home improvements, communications and financial services, even steamy love novels personalized with customers' names. Direct marketers use such methods as *direct* (door-to-door) *selling; direct-response retailing*, in which items are advertised in periodicals and on radio and television, with toll-free (800) telephone numbers available for placing orders; and *data-base marketing*, which offers lists of prospective customers to organizations, direct-mail firms, and telemarketing agencies, which contact potential consumers by phone.

Direct marketing is conducted by firms that sell their own products directly to the public and by those who sell the products of other companies. Direct-mail firms and telemarketing agencies are employed by both large and small manufacturers. Telemarketing alone is a roughly $100-billion-a-year industry with an annual growth rate of 30 percent. Many companies employ a *telemarketing director* and *telesales representatives* to offer their products for sale over the telephone or to set up appointments for visits by company sales representatives. A variety of career opportunities exist in direct marketing. Some require no formal education and pay roughly minimum wage and perhaps bonuses. Others in management require college degrees in business, marketing, or related areas.

International Marketing

The field of international marketing holds much fascination for those with an interest in travel and foreign countries. The growing import-export business and the global economy resulting from more and more free trade agreements among countries have increased opportunities in this field. As more businesses become involved in international marketing by establishing foreign operations or entering joint ventures with foreign companies, more positions become available. Other ways in which companies enter foreign markets are through exporting their products or making foreign licensing arrangements through which a company allows a foreign firm to produce and market its product in exchange for royalties.

The growth in international marketing due to changes abroad will create more positions based in the United States for individuals interested in international marketing. However, entry-level positions abroad are few. Travel and assignments abroad usually are associated with high-level managers; managers or owners of advertising agencies with operations abroad; owners of import-export businesses; sales representatives of industrial or pharmaceutical companies; and fashion coordinators and buyers. Usually companies hire foreign nationals for most positions in foreign branches, a practice often required by the foreign country's government in allowing the company to do business there. Positions abroad for recent college graduates are rare, even for those with an MBA and knowledge of the local language, though this may change with the current growth level of international business.

Opportunities for students to live and work abroad can be arranged by AISEC, a student-run, nonprofit organization that sets up internships abroad lasting from 6 weeks to 18 months. Individuals interested in international marketing should become proficient in at least one foreign language and systematically collect information on the countries and industries of interest. Before being assigned a position abroad, marketing professionals are usually required to have a thorough knowledge of their firm's domestic marketing operations.

CAREER PATHS AND COMPENSATION

An understanding of the variety and quantity of different careers in marketing can be gleaned from the breadth of the marketing function itself. Career paths were discussed in greater detail as part of the job descriptions in the previous section. Figure 6-1 shows how marketing positions in a fairly large organization relate to one another, including salary ranges and mobility.

Corporate sales, where many marketing graduates begin, is an excellent position from which to start a career path that could lead right to the top of the organization. A recent *Business Week* survey of chief executive officers in the 1,000 top U.S. companies revealed that 27 percent came up through the merchandising-marketing ranks, second only to the 31 percent who advanced from finance-accounting.

The salary ranges in Figure 6-1 are estimates. Salaries differ from industry to industry in accordance with industry norms. For new graduates in marketing, average annual salaries may differ by a couple hundred dollars to over $3,000 for the same job, depending on location. Lowest salaries usually are found in the Southeast and highest salaries in the West. The cost of living may vary accordingly, explaining in part the salary differences.

Compensation packages contain more than salary alone, however. In response to employee demands, companies now are offering better and more varied benefit packages that differ in value. Fringe benefits may include health insurance, life insurance, disability compensation, vacation, sick and maternity leave, paid holidays, bonuses, pension plans, employee stock ownership and/or stock purchase plans, and profit-sharing plans. Job applicants must evaluate these benefits along with the salary to compute total compensation.

For top marketing executives in major national corporations, six-digit salaries are not unusual. Executive benefit packages are likely to include all of the aforementioned, plus chauffeur-driven limousines, country club memberships, and a range of personal and professional services.Most managers and supervisors receive profit-sharing benefits as additional incentives. Sales representatives can make six-digit incomes as well, when bonuses are added to salary and commissions.

For professionals in advertising, sales promotion, and public relations firms, entry-level salaries usually are lower than for comparable posi-

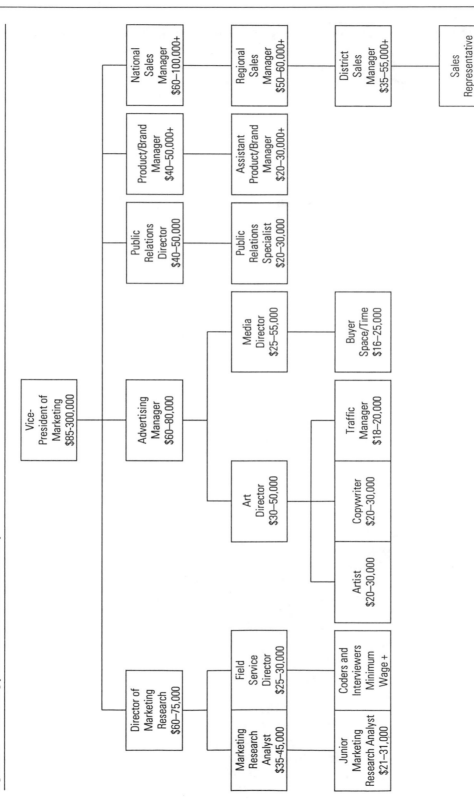

Figure 6-1   Marketing positions, salaries, and mobility

tions in large organizations, but as the professionals advance in these firms, salaries become relatively higher.

CURRENT TRENDS

Marketing occurs in an ever-changing environment to which marketing professionals must adapt. Many factors beyond their control impact their jobs. The U.S. economy is a postindustrial service economy. Within the next decade, 9 out of 10 new jobs will be in the service sector. Many new graduates entering the job market must be prepared to enter this service sector. The markets of the 1970s changed dramatically with the introduction of new technologies, the flood of imports, and deregulation in the airlines and other key industries. The 1980s became a decade of mergers and acquisitions as organizations attempted to remain profitable or grow through restructuring during these turbulent times. This upheaval created opportunities for entrepreneurs who found market niches or small groups of consumers with unfilled needs for specific goods or services. New small businesses in record numbers were created to meet these needs, hence the 1980s were characterized by an entrepreneurial boom. Chapter 10 describes opportunities for entrepreneurs, educators, and consultants.

Retail Trends

Two prevalent trends emerged in the retail industry during the 1980s: (1) the reshaping of large department stores as a result of mergers and acquisitions and (2) the emergence of specialty shops. The increasing number of working women has contributed to the success of these specialty shops, which offer the convenience of quick shopping with no lines. Changing lifestyles and values have made a dramatic impact on markets and products. The demand for fast food is becoming a demand for fast, *healthful* food as nutrition and fitness concerns grow. Change has fed the boom in new businesses, along with a reasonably strong economy in the 1980s. The weakened economy of the 1990s should slow down somewhat the development of new businesses and opportunities for entrepreneurs.

Global Marketing

Opportunities in international marketing will increase as firms respond to the invasion of imports with aggressive selling in foreign markets. As American business moves abroad, the need in all areas of marketing for individuals who are familiar with foreign languages and cultures will grow substantially. *Global marketing* will be the key term in the 1990s and people who are prepared to assume a role in it will find excellent career possibilities, though not usually abroad.

Environmental Concerns

Preservation of the environment became a strong political issue in the late 1980s. This widely held concern has affected product development, manufacturing processes, and packaging. Products now are advertised to emphasize nonpollutance, and recyclable or recycled materials are used in the products and their containers. Paper and glass have begun to regain some popularity lost to plastics. Many plastic bags are now somewhat bio-degradable, and most plastic products now carry a code number for the recycling process. Concern for endangered species and rain forests also have become international environmental issues. Institutions have been shaken. Bob Barker, a game-show host and animal-rights activist, withdrew from participation in the Miss Universe pageant over the issue of fur coats that were to be awarded as prizes. Even the pencil—widely made from jelutong, a wood that grows in the rain forests of Indonesia and Malaysia—is part of a global controversy. Groups such as Rainforest Action Network and performers such as rock musician Sting urge preservation of the rain forests in the ongoing fight to reduce deterioration of the ozone layer.

A move to highlight the environmental safety message resulted in green labeling of products "friendly" to the environment, including those that are biodegradable, manufactured without polluting, or enclosed in recyclable packaging. Although this type of labeling is often confusing to consumers, more and more companies are modifying both products and containers rather than risk boycotts of their products by consumer groups. Recently, the H. J. Heinz Company agreed to a dolphin protection plan in the process of netting tuna for its Star-Kist brand. Although a boycott sponsored by the Earth Island Institute had not yet hurt sales, the company felt that being branded the largest slaughterer of dolphins in the world did damage the company's image. According to a recent survey conducted by Opinion Research Corporation in Princeton, N.J., 27 percent of the consumers queried claimed that they have boycotted a product because of the manufacturer's record on the environment. Today's marketers have found that it is good business to recognize consumer interests and to address environmental issues.

Superagencies

Megamergers among advertising agencies have resulted in 20 "super-agencies," half of which are controlled by five holding companies. These agencies offer a broader range of services to clients and on a global scale. Tomorrow's job applicants in advertising face a more stable environment but a highly competitive job market.

JOB OPPORTUNITIES

A huge field, marketing employed over 9 million American workers in 1986 and is predicted to employ over 12 million in the year 2000, according to the U.S. Bureau of Labor Statistics. In addition, by the end of 1988, over 19.6 million workers were employed in retail sales. Of this number, 35 percent were part time. Marketing professionals are employed throughout the United States by manufacturers, retailers, advertising agencies, consulting and public relations firms, product testing laboratories, business services firms, and others.

Demand
While demand for new college graduates varies from position to position and from industry to industry, recent studies show that of all new graduates, the demand for those in marketing/sales is the third-greatest of all areas. Still, competition for many entry-level positions can be quite keen.

One study identified the hottest careers in 1988; six were directly related to marketing. At the top of the list were corporate real estate managers, followed by service quality managers. Ranked ninth was export manager for international marketing. Number 13 was private-label manager in the field of fashion merchandising. Sixteenth was sports marketer, whose responsibilities include handling sports-related special events, sponsorships, promotions, and advertising. High-tech public relations manager was in slot 20.

Though job openings in most areas of marketing will grow at a faster-than-average rate, graduates seeking jobs in such areas as marketing research, advertising, sales promotion, and public relations will meet stiff competition. Major growth in the marketing field is occurring in independent research, advertising, public relations and other services firms, consistent with the trend toward contracting out certain business activities. Bureau of Labor Statistics growth projections from 1986 to 2000 for various marketing careers are as follows:

Table 6.1

Career	Percentage of growth
Advertising managers	30
Economists and marketing research anaylsts	34
Manufacturing sales	3
Public relations specialists	40
Retail sales	32
Service sales	56
Visual artists	30
Wholesale sales	33

APTITUDES AND ATTRIBUTES NEEDED FOR SUCCESS

The spectrum of marketing careers provides diverse opportunities for individuals with a range of different educational backgrounds, skills, aptitudes, and interests. More than any other area of business, marketing offers jobs for artistic, communications, quantitative, and entrepreneurial types. It is important to understand, however, the unique requirements for success in each area and to know in which areas competition for jobs will be particularly fierce. In these areas, experience as well as talent and educational background will play an important part in landing a good job.

Education and Personal Characteristics
Retail Sales. A high school diploma is adequate for finding a position in retail sales. Indeed, many students still in high school find part time sales positions. The successful retail salesperson needs an ability to communicate well with customers and a knowledge of the products in the department. A salesperson may be promoted to a supervisory position with

no more than a high school diploma, but if you set your sights on a position as buyer or department manager, a college degree in merchandising, marketing, management, or a related business area is almost always required. The more knowledge you acquire through formal education, the better your chances of advancing in retailing.

Wholesale and Industrial Sales. In wholesale and industrial sales, high school graduates may work in the stockroom or shipping department, but it is unlikely that they will ever advance into sales. As professionalism grows in wholesale and industrial sales, as products become increasingly more complex and competition stiffer, and as the use of high-tech equipment for more effective selling becomes widespread, sales positions usually will go to college graduates. New college graduates may enter sales directly out of school, but they face competition from experienced sales personnel who leave retail sales jobs for greater salaries and advancement possibilities. Technical knowledge is necessary for those selling electronics, machinery, chemicals, and pharmaceuticals. Though companies provide training, candidates with knowledge or experience in these areas tend to get the jobs.

If you are interested in wholesale and industrial sales, a degree in business provides a good general background. In many technical areas such as electronics and pharmaceuticals, the best jobs go to candidates with technical undergraduate degrees and courses in business or an MBA. Students should choose an industry of interest and gain as much knowledge of that industry as possible while still in college. (The subject of choosing an industry will be discussed in Chapter 11.) Some basic attributes leading to success in wholesale and industrial sales include the ability to communicate well with people, the knowledge of how to organize and manage your time, the persistence to follow through, personal initiative, reliability on the job, creativity, and—most important—a positive attitude toward selling—without that, forget it!

Marketing Research and Marketing Management. In these areas both undergraduate degrees in marketing or management and sometimes graduate-level business degrees are essential. Undergraduate degrees in marketing, statistics, or economics are usual entry-level requirements. In addition, the MBA is preferred by many employers because of the broad knowledge of business that it provides, especially in product management. Marketing research is one area, unlike most other marketing areas, in which formal education plays a large part. Courses in psychology provide the background for motivational research, and courses in sociology provide information on how societal influences affect the buying practices of consumers. Knowledge in both areas is essential, along with the ability to use computers and statistical methods to conduct research and the organizational and writing skills to write proposals and reports.

Helpful personal attributes are logical thought processes, curiosity, problem-solving ability, and a pleasant interviewing style. If you have the impression that the marketing researcher who ultimately becomes the research director must be good in all areas, you are exactly right. That's what makes getting ahead in this area a real challenge. For those who aspire to management positions, outstanding performance in the marketing area of their choice, along with graduate work in business and marketing, is essential. Let your education enhance your personal strengths to help you succeed.

Advertising, Sales Promotion, and Public Relations. Advertising, sales promotion, and public relations are also areas in which personal attributes and special abilities play the most important role in success. A good background in marketing or communications is certainly helpful, but it will not guarantee you the job you want. Competition for the sought-after positions in these areas comes from majors in English, psychology, sociology, and a variety of other areas.

Your educational background should instill in you a knowledge of major concepts of the field, a familiarity with sources of information, the habit of reading and keeping up-to-date, and the ability to make better decisions— but that's only part of it. Creativity, artistic ability, excellent communication skills, insights into people, and willingness to take risks by putting your ideas on the line are essential for success.

For creative jobs, normally portfolios with samples of work are required. One of the best ways to gain experience and to test abilities for work in advertising, sales promotion, and public relations is through internships and part-time jobs.

Internships

A good source of information on internships found in many college career centers is *Internships in Advertising, Marketing, Public Relations, & Sales* published by The Career Press, Inc., P.O. Box 34, Hawthorne, NJ 07507. Internships are offered during summer, winter recesses, and regular school terms. Not all interns receive pay; those who do earn on average $200 to $300 per week. Because internships are such a desirable way to break into marketing fields, competition for them is often stiff. An applicant's best chance of landing one is to develop a good resume, target an interest area, and use all available resources to get leads on internships.

Competition

Many young advertising professionals launch their careers through participation in the InterAd competition. Twice a year, the American Graduate School in International Management holds competitions in which student teams create complete marketing and advertising campaigns for launching real products into international markets. Corporate sponsors such as AT&T and Eastman Kodak Company provide the teams with $5,000 to cover research costs and production materials. The competition is judged by advertising agency and marketing executives across the country who may then interview competing students for jobs in their agencies or companies.

For those interested in international business, the school offers a program of study requiring from 12 to 18 months to complete. Approximately 900 students per year graduate with a master's in international management, which makes them more competitive in vying for jobs in international marketing.

SOURCES OF ADDITIONAL INFORMATION

Much information on careers in marketing is available in university career centers and libraries. General timely information on marketing fields can be found in such periodicals as *Advertising Age, Adweek/Marketing Week, Journal of Marketing, Journal of Marketing Research, Marketing and Media Decisions, Public Relations Journal*, and dozens of others.

For specific career information, you can write to professional marketing associations. The American Marketing Association offers an entire bibliography of sources and a placement service for marketing graduates. The American Advertising Federation provides a list of colleges that offer programs in advertising and is an excellent source of advertising internships offered by many of its members. The addresses of these and other associations are listed below.

American Advertising Federation
1400 K Street N.W., Suite 1000
Washington, DC 20005

American Association of
    Advertising Agencies
666 Third Avenue, 13th Floor
New York, NY 10017

American Marketing Association
250 S. Wacker Drive
Chicago, IL 60606

American Retail Federation
1616 H Street N.W.
Washington, DC 20006

American Telemarketing
    Association
5000 Van Nuys Boulevard, #400
Sherman Oaks, CA 91403

Direct Marketing Association
11 W. 42nd Street
New York, NY 10036-8096

International Trade Council
1900 Mt. Vernon Avenue
P.O. Box 2478
Alexandria, VA 22301-0478

Manufacturers' Agents National
    Association
23016 Mill Creek Road
P.O. Box 3467
Laguna Hills, CA 92654

Marketing Research Association
111 E. Wacker Drive, Suite 600
Chicago, IL 60601

"Employment and Career
Opportunities in Marketing
Research," a free publication,
is offered by the Marketing
Research Association.

National Association of Service Merchandising
221 N. LaSalle Street
Chicago, IL 60601

National Association of Wholesalers and Distributors
1725 K Street N.W.
Washington, DC 20006

National Council of Salesmen's Organizations
222 Broadway, Room 515
New York, NY 10007

National Retail Merchants Association
100 W. 31st Street
New York, NY 10001

Product Development and Management Association
c/o Thomas P. Hustad

Indiana University Graduate School of Business
801 W. Michigan Street
Indianapolis, IN 46202-5151

Promotion Marketing Association of America
322 Eighth Avenue, Suite 1201
New York, NY 10001

Pi Sigma Epsilon
155 E. Capitol Drive
Hartland, WI 53029

(Students may obtain career and scholarship information from this sales fraternity associated with SMEI.)

Public Relations Society of America
33 Irving Place, 3rd Floor
New York, NY 10003

(This organization has a student branch, Public Relations Student Society of America.)

Sales and Marketing Executives International (SMEI)
Statler Office Tower, 458
Cleveland, OH 44115

The Advertising Club of New York
155 East 55th Street, Suite 202
New York, NY 10022

(This organization has a Young Professionals Division for individuals under 30 or having fewer than two years of experience.)

The Council of Sales Promotion Agencies
750 Summer Street, 2nd Floor
Stamford, CT 06901

CAREER DECISION-MAKING MODEL

It is now time to consider a career in marketing. Figure 6-2 is a form with the factors included from the career decision-making model described in greater detail in Chapter 1. Follow these directions in completing it.

1. Enter the position that interests you most on the line titled *Job*.
2. Enter any additional factors used to personalize your model (from Chapter 1) in the blank spaces provided.
3. Enter the weights that you assigned to the factors (from Chapter 1) in the column *WT*. (It would be wise to review the explanations of the factors in the description of the model in Chapter 1 before on to step 4.)
4. Assign a value from 1 (lowest) to 10 (highest) to each factor based on the information in this chapter and on your personal self-assessment, entering the value in the column *V*. If you feel that you have a certain aptitude or attribute needed for success in this career area, you should assign a fairly high value. If a certain interest, such as amount of variety, is desirable to you and you feel the area provides the variety you enjoy, assign a fairly high value. If not, assign a low value. Use this technique to assign values to all factors in the model. If you cannot assign a value based on the information in the chapter for some of the factors in the model, either use other sources to acquire the information or leave the space beside the factor blank.
5. Multiply the weight times the value entering the score in the column *S*.
6. Add the scores in column S for each group of factors entering the number in the space labeled *Total*.

You will use this evaluation in Chapter 11 in combination with evaluations of each career explored in this book.

WHAT DID YOU LEARN?

This chapter included a lot of information on careers in marketing. Now you know what kind of work marketing professionals do, who employs them, what kinds of salaries they earn, the career paths that many of them follow, what the job outlook is, what trends are affecting it, how to prepare yourself for a marketing career, and where to find additional information. You completed a career evaluation for marketing.

Chapter 7, "Careers in Operations, Production, and Materials Management," will give you a look at the behind-the-scenes professionals in manufacturing firms.

Figure 6-2 Career evaluation for marketing

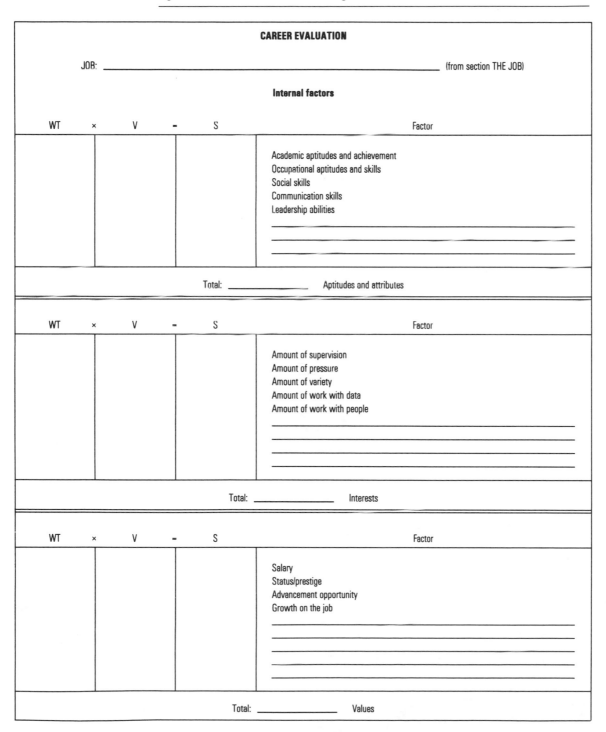

CAREER EVALUATION

JOB: _____ (from section THE JOB)

Internal factors

WT	×	V	=	S	Factor
					Academic aptitudes and achievement
					Occupational aptitudes and skills
					Social skills
					Communication skills
					Leadership abilities

Total: _____ Aptitudes and attributes

WT	×	V	=	S	Factor
					Amount of supervision
					Amount of pressure
					Amount of variety
					Amount of work with data
					Amount of work with people

Total: _____ Interests

WT	×	V	=	S	Factor
					Salary
					Status/prestige
					Advancement opportunity
					Growth on the job

Total: _____ Values

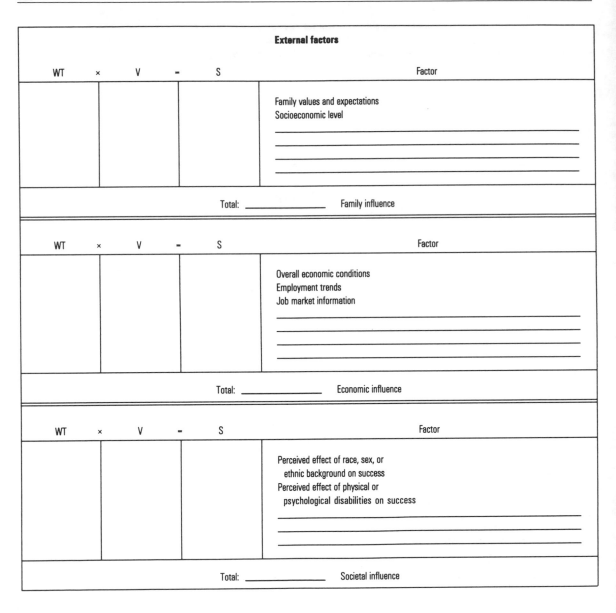

WT	×	V	–	S	Factor
					External factors

Family values and expectations
Socioeconomic level

Total: _____ Family influence

Overall economic conditions
Employment trends
Job market information

Total: _____ Economic influence

Perceived effect of race, sex, or
  ethnic background on success
Perceived effect of physical or
  psychological disabilities on success

Total: _____ Societal influence

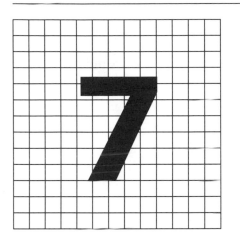

CAREERS IN OPERATIONS, PRODUCTION, AND MATERIALS MANAGEMENT

CHAPTER OBJECTIVES

Upon completion of this chapter, you should be able to:

1. Describe the work of production managers, line supervisors, manufacturing managers, production planners, quality assurance managers, operations research analysts, materials managers, purchasing managers, purchasing agents, buyers, expediters, traffic managers, and inventory managers.

2. Discuss trends in operations, production, and materials management and their impact on careers.

3. Diagram career paths for workers in operations, production, and materials management.

4. Discuss job opportunities in the fields of operations, production, and materials management today.

5. List the educational preparation and skills needed for positions in operations, production, and materials management.

6. Evaluate careers in operations, production, and materials management according to your individualized career decision-making model.

As American business moves from the industrial to the information age, the most substantial and dramatic impact is on the U.S. manufacturing firm. While the service-producing sector expands rapidly, the manufacturing sector will create only one of every six jobs. In addition, continued competition from foreign manufacturing firms at home and abroad, expanded use of technology, and increased demand for better-quality products have created other changes in what, how, and where American manufacturing is done. As a result, production management is one of the hot career fields of the 1990s.

Production is the area within manufacturing that is least glamorized but most essential. It involves procuring materials to produce a product and planning and controlling the manufacturing process. Materials management is concerned with all activities in the procurement and distribution of materials needed to manufacture a product. After the materials are obtained, the production begins and after production, distribution of the product. The term *operations management* is used widely today to include managing the production of goods or services. Such operations concepts as job design, facility location, capacity planning, work force management, inventory, and scheduling fall into this category.

The organizational structure and operations of each industry and manufacturing firm vary as it produces its products. The objective is to work effectively and efficiently to assure quality. This work is the responsibility of employees in the manufacturing function. This chapter will give you a fairly general and comprehensive look at operations and production careers. Included is such information as:

- what jobs production personnel perform
- who employs these professionals
- salaries and career paths
- latest trends
- job opportunities
- education and skills needed to pursue production careers
- sources of additional information

THE JOB: OPERATIONS AND PRODUCTION MANAGEMENT

The vice-president of operations/production, the regional managers, and the individual plant managers are all *production managers* working at different levels of responsibility. They are involved with production planning and control for the company nationwide, for a certain region, or for an individual plant, respectively. Production is the technical side of management and makes use of quantitative tools and computers to determine the material requirements for production, the most efficient way to manufacture a product, and how to control for quality. Production involves the management of personnel and machines.

An entry-level production job for a college graduate is *line supervisor*. The responsibility of the line supervisor is to oversee the people who run the machines. Many line supervisors are responsible for scheduling production runs, designing budgets, and maintaining employee relations. An individual may be moved a number of times to varied positions before advancing to *manufacturing manager*, head of the entire manufacturing operation.

Such staff positions as *production planner* might be held by upwardly mobile production management candidates. Production planners prepare production schedules for manufacturing industrial and commercial products. They may also be responsible for planning new plant layouts, projecting inventory levels, and calculating long-term expenditures for facilities and equipment.

A staff production job that a beginner might be assigned is *assistant quality assurance manager*. This assistant works closely with the *quality assurance manager*, assuming some of the responsibility for preventing product deficiencies and detecting and correcting any that do exist. The quality assurance manager and staff review a product's design requirements and often participate in the selection of materials and suppliers. The manager directs sampling, inspecting, and testing operations and sets standards for the rejection of defective parts. Working as part of the quality assurance staff are *engineers*, *technicians*, and *inspectors*.

Another important staff position in the production process is that of the *operations research* (OR) *analyst*. The OR analyst is a specialist who uses mathematical tools and computer technology to analyze business operations, methods, and products to provide information to the managers who must make sound decisions. Usually the operations research analyst reports to executives fairly high up in the company and deals with solutions to large, complex problems. An analyst might be responsible for planning a production schedule that keeps the cost of production and inventory low and eliminates the piling up of unfilled orders. Many college management programs offer a program in operations and production that combines operations research techniques with production knowledge. However, the work of operations analysts is performed in all large organizations and in all functional areas, not only in production.

THE JOB: MATERIALS MANAGEMENT

The *materials manager* has an important function in the production process. Basically, materials management involves having the right item, at the right place, at the right time, at a reasonable cost. This is true for manufacturers of both goods and services. The emphasis in service firms is ordering, receiving, storing, and distributing within the firm the supplies required to perform the service. In manufacturing firms, the materials management function is extended to include not only management of materials needed to produce the product, but also storing the product throughout all phases of production and in its finished form; moving the product to the shipping department; and transporting the product to distribution centers, warehouses, or directly to customers.

Responsible in many organizations for the procurement, storage, and movement of materials within the company, the materials managers must be industry specialists. They keep the production manager posted on the industry's current capabilities, emerging technology, and individual suppliers and their products. The major task of materials managers is the identification of suppliers breaking significant new ground in materials and production technology. Materials and purchasing managers interact regularly with engineering and quality control professionals.

Working under the materials manager are a group of purchasing professionals. The primary purchasing functions are establishing sources of supply, getting the needed items on order, setting prices and delivery dates, and dealing with shortages. Purchasing, though sometimes underrated, is extremely important. There are two aspects of profit—making money and reducing costs. Shrewd buying at good prices in this time of inflation and shortages has established the *purchasing manager* as an integral part of the management team. The purchasing manager is responsible for establishing and enforcing purchasing department policies, forecasting supply and price trends, seeking new ideas and sources of materials, recommending that specific materials and components be used in production, and participating in new product development with respect to projected costs.

Working under the supervision of the purchasing manager are the *purchasing agents*. Usually purchasing agents are involved both in buying personally and in supervising the buying activities of assistant purchasing agents and buyers. Depending on the size of the purchasing department, senior purchasing agents may do more or less buying and supervising. For example, in a large department, a purchasing agent may do less buying and more training, development, and supervision of subordinates.

The job of the *buyer* involves such responsibilities as placing orders with suppliers, checking the progress of overdue orders, conducting interviews with industrial salespersons to consider new materials, and keeping close contact with suppliers through correspondence, phone calls, and plant visits. The buyer must be good at cost/price analysis—that is, able to judge the fairness of a supplier's quoted price by judging what the supplier's costs are. The successful buyer maintains an effective number of sources and always has a backup supplier for necessary items. To be able to take advantage of opportunities to stock up on items that may run short or that are offered at a good price, the buyer must always be aware of market conditions. Building long-term supplier relationships often assures good prices and on-time deliveries. These relationships measure the success of the buyer.

Many buyers specialize, depending on the company or industry in which they are employed. Such specialty areas include raw material or commodity buying; production material or component buying; construction buying, which may involve negotiations for buildings, facilities, or major equipment; maintenance materials, tools, spare parts, and operating supplies buying; and general-purpose buying of a wide range of materials generally of low value. These last two specialty areas are typical initial assignments and do not require the technical expertise of the other three areas.

Many start careers in purchasing in the position of *expediter*. The responsibility of the expediter is to see that delivery commitments made by suppliers are kept or, if delays occur, to attempt to speed the deliveries. This job, although clerical in nature, has expanded as companies are seeking to reduce time between order and delivery of materials. As expediter, a beginner has an opportunity to become familiar with most items purchased as well as who supplies them—the necessary background for advancing to an assistant buyer position.

After materials are purchased, the traffic function comes into play. The *traffic manager* deals mainly with securing delivery of purchased materials. Responsibilities for overall supervision of traffic operations—which include quoting freight rates to buyers, procuring special cars and equipment for transporting materials, handling claims and adjustments on damaged shipments, routing and tracing inbound shipments, and approving transportation bills—are handled by the traffic manager. In larger companies, the traffic manager heads a separate department; in smaller companies, the traffic function may be part of the purchasing department.

A final aspect of the materials management picture is inventory control. The *inventory manager* is responsible for maintaining in storage the levels of inventory necessary for the production process. Working closely with the purchasing and traffic managers, the inventory manager has an important role in seeing that materials scheduled for use are available in inventory.

CAREER PATHS AND COMPENSATION

There is room for advancement in all areas of operations and production for those with drive, ability, and the proper educational background. In manufacturing firms, production is considered the most critical function. It is no surprise, then, that production managers earn excellent salaries and have a good shot at the chief executive position. The vice-president of production is one step from the top.

Today, advancement and salary within operations/production management are determined not only by the ability to make critical decisions, but also by technical knowledge and experience. Many of the critical decisions involve using technology, such as robots, in the production process. Also, much of the information used by production personnel to monitor the production process is available via computer and telecommunication systems. The greater technical expertise production managers have, the greater their value to their organizations.

Depending on the degree of importance placed on materials and the way the firm is structured, materials management may prove to be a direct route to the top. Some firms may assign a vice-president of materials who functions at the same level as the production vice-president. Because of the growing importance of the purchasing function and the necessary role of the materials manager in market forecasting, production planning, and inventory control, the materials orientation in firms has increased.

Notice Figure 7-1. Clearly the purchasing manager is in line for the materials management position, but not without competition. To advance from purchasing to materials management, an individual must gain a deeper knowledge of the operations of other departments and be proficient in the use of computers and quantitative techniques. This necessary knowledge makes manufacturing line managers and quality assurance specialists viable candidates for a move into the key materials management slot.

The college graduate interested in a purchasing career should seek immediate placement in the purchasing department as an assistant buyer or even an assistant purchasing agent, although movement into purchasing from other areas within the company is frequent. According to the March 1991 issue of the *College Placement Council Salary Survey*, new bachelor's degree candidates received, on average, salary offers of $24,787 a year for beginning purchasing positions. Applicants with high school diplomas or community college degrees may start off as expediters or stock clerks or perhaps assistant buyers in the case of the applicant who holds an AA degree and has some technical background.

There are public purchasing positions available in government, hospitals, and educational institutions. Salaries are a bit lower than in private industry. In addition to the slightly higher salaries in the private sector, the majority of companies offer bonuses to purchasing personnel.

The quality assurance manager usually has spent a number of years in supervision at a lower level somewhere in production to gain the experience in administration and planning needed to advance to the position of manager.

The greater emphasis on strategic planning and critical decision making in manufacturing firms, coupled with advanced technology, have catapulted the operations research analyst into a position of major importance. A top operations research analyst in a large corporation can earn as much as $150,000 a year, according to an article in the June 1990 issue of *Money* magazine. Greater recognition, greater salary, greater risks, and greater opportunity to move into top management positions are all characteristics of positions in operations research.

As you observe the salaries in Figure 7-1, be aware that these figures are extrapolated from past salary surveys and are therefore estimates.

CURRENT TRENDS

The global economy has significantly affected American manufacturing firms. John Naisbitt well documented Japanese assertiveness in his book *The Year Ahead, 1986*. Japanese firms into the 1990s are making investments in American firms, opening their own manufacturing plants within the United States, employing over 100,000 American workers in their operations, and participating in joint ventures with American firms. In addition, American firms are competing with low-cost, high-quality imports from other countries. Several U.S. firms are having to open plants abroad, improve quality control operations, and shorten the time materials remain in inventory to compete effectively in both the national and international marketplace.

Technology has both eliminated and created industries and careers in manufacturing. Over the past decade, many manufacturing workers were replaced by robots. On the other hand, the robotics industry is expected to increase the number of robotic manufacturing plants to 44,500

Figure 7-1 Operations/Production positions, salaries, and mobility

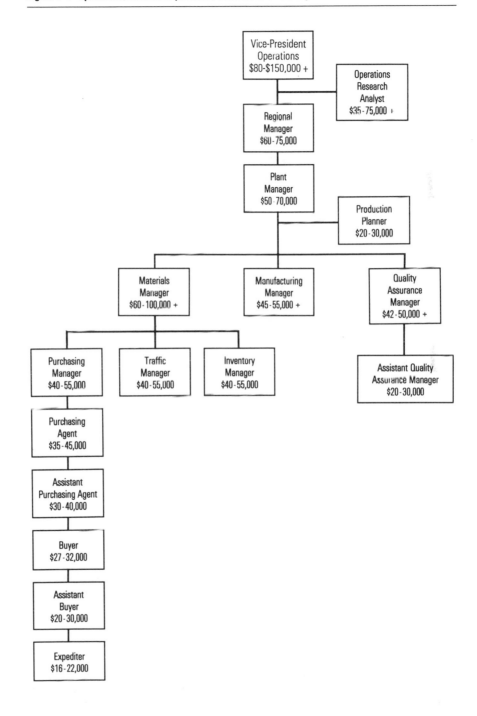

by 1995. Similar growth is expected in the related fiber optics, laser, and telecommunications industries. The new jobs created by these industries will require higher technical levels of training than the old assembly line jobs.

The use of robots with computer technology has created computer-aided manufacturing (CAM) and computer-aided design (CAD). Some organizations have integrated some of the production processes with computers, termed computer-integrated manufacturing (CIM), while other organizations have the entire manufacturing process controlled and performed by computers (Flexible Manufacturing System). Expansion of existing systems through artificial intelligence (AI) and expert systems should continue in the future, thus changing the manufacturing function even more.

Computerization also has changed the nature of purchasing occupations but has not eliminated jobs. With less paperwork, purchasing agents and managers can spend more time on buying decisions. Computers facilitate accessing up-to-date product and price listings, maintaining desired inventory levels, processing orders, and determining when to place orders. There is a trend today toward limited-source contracting, in which purchasing agents deal with fewer suppliers, having identified those who offer the overall best quality, service, and price.

Implications of these technological changes are worth considering. Employees within manufacturing firms will need to continue to develop new skills. New training and retraining will increase for employees. Managers will operate differently within the production function.

JOB OPPORTUNITIES

Demand

Overall, career opportunities in operations and production areas are increasing at an average rate through the year 2000, according to Bureau of Labor statistics. Industrial production managers are expected to increase in number by 39,000 (18 percent) from 1988 to the year 2000 with increased production of consumer and industrial products. Jobs in purchasing provide especially ample opportunities. Growth in the purchasing profession is influenced by the inflation and scarce resource conditions that prevail today.

Approximately 458,000 purchasing agents and managers were employed in 1988. It is estimated that by the year 2000, positions will increase by 14 percent. Opportunities for purchasing positions occur in government agencies, hospitals, and educational institutions, but over half of the opportunities occur in manufacturing industries. Half of all purchasing agents work in small departments with fewer than five employees. There is excellent demand for MBAs and business, science, or engineering graduates with a couple of courses in purchasing. There are also ample opportunities for graduates of two-year programs, but these opportunities are mostly limited to small firms. Especially high demand is for individuals with technical backgrounds to work in companies that manufacture complex items such as industrial engines and electronics equipment.

Another area in which demand is strong and continuous is quality assurance. The use of increasingly complex products and production methods, combined with ever more stringent government regulations, has contributed to the growth in job opportunities in the area of quality assurance. This increasing complexity in industrial operations and the expansion of automated processes have also resulted in moderate growth in opportunities for production planners.

Finally, a young and rapidly growing profession is operations research analysis. The job opportunities for OR analysts are predicted to increase by 30,000 (55.4 percent) from 1988 to 2000. Operations research analysts are employed in increasing numbers by large organizations including local, state, and federal governments, the military, public services, and private industry. Most new opportunities will be in manufacturing, trade, and service firms. Some analysts have doctorates and work for research foundations or universities.

Equal opportunity standing

Opportunities in production and materials management are expected to increase for women and members of minority racial or ethnic groups. The December 23, 1985, issue of *U.S. News and World Report* documented a fiber optics plant in which the work force was one-third female and one-quarter minority. Because less physical strength is needed with the newer technologies, more production opportunities are expected for women. For many minorities, their opportunities may depend on obtaining training or retraining to compete for new positions.

For any workers aspiring to the top executive position in a company, a recent *Business Week* survey of chief executive officers at the 1,000 most valuable U.S. companies revealed that 11 percent came up through the production-manufacturing ranks. Thus, advancement possibilities are limitless.

APTITUDES AND ATTRIBUTES NEEDED FOR SUCCESS

Production Management

Education. A production planner may be selected from manufacturing, engineering, and machine shop departments. Usually on-the-job training is available. Some employers require a degree in business or engineering with knowledge of data processing. Usually a college degree is not required unless a production planner wants to advance to a management position.

In the area of quality assurance, an associate degree is a good background for a position as quality assurance technician or inspector. Movement into management requires additional education. Usual requirements for advancement to quality assurance manager are an undergraduate degree in engineering or science and an MBA. Also acceptable is a business undergraduate degree with courses in science. Industrial experience is always required. Critical to the effectiveness of a quality assurance manager is the ability to work with all levels of personnel from the production worker to the top executive.

The minimum education for those interested in operations research is a BS in math, engineering, operations management, or economics. Several math courses above calculus as well as a knowledge of probability theory, statistics, and computers are required. An excellent background for a position as operations research analyst in private industry is a bachelor's degree in math and an MBA.

Personal characteristics. To be a successful operations research analyst requires some unique skills and attributes. Included are the abilities to:

- think logically
- be creative
- formulate problems
- identify stumbling blocks in a project
- find available resources
- recognize restrictions

Materials Management

Personal characteristics. Purchasing managers, agents, and buyers spend millions of dollars of their companies' money each year. Because of this economic power, they are often under pressure to bend the rules for kickbacks or other favors. For this reason, a high degree of ethics is essential for purchasing professionals. In general, effective purchasing pros tend to have a more positive self-image, excellent communication abilities, strong professional interests, and a preference for jobs providing opportunities for variety, challenge, and professional growth. Knowledge in the areas of contract formulation, data processing, and hedging techniques that avoid risk by trading in commodity futures is desirable and can be gained in such classes as economics, accounting, purchasing, finance, management, and data processing.

Education. Although the educational requirements vary somewhat from company to company, most firms prefer to hire college graduates with degrees in business. Other degree holders are considered, but some business courses usually are required. Most large companies prefer applicants with MBAs. For companies that manufacture complex machinery or chemicals, an undergraduate degree in engineering or science with an MBA is most desirable.

A four-year college degree is not necessary, however, for entry into purchasing careers. A high school graduate may be hired in a clerical or stockroom position and move into purchasing work as the employee gains knowledge and experience. Smaller companies readily hire graduates with associate degrees for entry-level purchasing jobs, but for movement into management, a bachelor's degree is important regardless of the size of the company.

Certification.   Two certification programs exist for purchasing professionals today. For those in private industry, the certified purchasing manager (CPM) certificate is conferred by the National Association of Purchasing Management, Inc., after an applicant has passed four exams and acquired experience in purchasing. For those in public purchasing, the certified public purchasing officer (CPPO) certificate is conferred by the National Institute of Governmental Purchasing, Inc., after an applicant has passed three exams and acquired experience in purchasing. Although these certificates are no guarantee of better jobs or higher salaries today, it is likely that, with the upgrading of the profession, they will pay off in the future. Formal courses are offered by local association groups and many colleges to help individuals prepare for the exams.

SOURCES OF ADDITIONAL INFORMATION

There is much information available through the many organizations for operations, production, and materials management professionals. Listed below are the names and addresses of organizations to which you may write for career information.

For careers in production planning, write:

American Production and
  Inventory Control Society
500 W. Annandale Road
Falls Church, VA 22046

National Association of
  Manufacturing
1331 Pennsylvania Avenue, N.W.
Suite 1500 N.
Washington, DC 20004

For careers in quality assurance, write:

American Society for Quality
  Control
310 W. Wisconsin Avenue
Milwaukee, WI 53203

For careers in physical distribution, write:

Council of Logistics Management
2803 Butterfield Road, Suite 380
Oak Brook, IL 60521

For careers in operations research, write:

Mathematical Association of
  America
1529 18th Street N.W.
Washington, DC 20036
Operations Research Society of
  America
Mount Royal & Guilford Avenues
Baltimore, MD 21202

Society for Industrial and
  Applied Mathematics
3600 University City Science
  Center
Philadelphia, PA 19104-2688

For careers in purchasing, write the following:

National Association of
  Purchasing Management
2055 E. Centennial Circle
P. O. Box 22160
Tempe, AZ 85282
National Association of State
  Purchasing Officials
Box 11910
Lexington, KY 40578

National Institute of
  Governmental Purchasing, Inc.
115 Hillwood Avenue
Falls Church, VA 22046

CAREER DECISION-MAKING MODEL

Do these careers in operations and production interest you? Figure 7.2 is
a form with the factors included from the career decision-making model
in Chapter 1. Follow these directions in completing it.

1. Enter the position that interests you most on the line titled *Job*.
2. Enter any additional factors used to personalize your model
   (from Chapter 1) in the blank spaces provided.
3. Enter the weights that you assigned to the factors (from Chapter
   1) in the column *WT*. (It would be wise to review the explanations
   of the factors in the description of the model in Chapter 1 before
   going on to Step 4.)
4. Assign a value from 1 (lowest) to 10 (highest) to each factor based
   on the information in this chapter and on your personal self-
   assessment entering the value in the column *V*. If you feel that
   you have a certain aptitude or attribute needed for success in this
   career area, you should assign a fairly high value. If a certain interest, such as amount of variety, is desirable to you and you feel
   the area provides the variety you enjoy, assign a fairly high value.
   If not, assign a low value. Use this technique to assign values to all
   factors in the model. If you cannot assign a value based on the information in the chapter for some of the factors in the model, ei-

ther use other sources to acquire the information or leave the space beside the factor blank.

5. Multiply the weight times the value entering the score in the column *S*.

6. Add the scores in column S for each group of factors entering the number in the space labeled *Total*.

You will use this evaluation in Chapter 11 in combination with evaluations of each career explored in this book.

WHAT DID YOU LEARN?

You learned about the various careers in operations, production, and materials management in this chapter. Now you know what jobs are involved, what salaries can be earned, what some of the trends are, what the job outlook is, what education and skills are required to enter production and materials management careers, and where to get additional information. You completed the career evaluation model for operations, production, and materials management.

In Chapter 8, "Careers in Human Resource Management," you will explore the people-oriented area that is growing in scope and importance.

Figure 7-2 Career evaluation for operations, production, and materials management

CAREER EVALUATION

JOB: _____ (from section THE JOB)

Internal factors

WT	×	V	=	S	Factor
					Academic aptitudes and achievement Occupational aptitudes and skills Social skills Communication skills Leadership abilities

Total: _____ Aptitudes and attributes

WT	×	V	=	S	Factor
					Amount of supervision Amount of pressure Amount of variety Amount of work with data Amount of work with people

Total: _____ Interests

WT	×	V	=	S	Factor
					Salary Status/prestige Advancement opportunity Growth on the job

Total: _____ Values

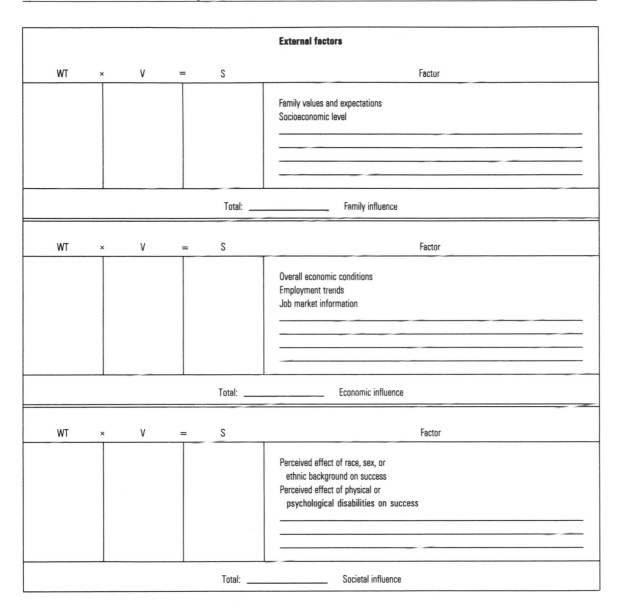

External factors

	WT × V = S	Factor

Family values and expectations
Socioeconomic level

Total: _____ Family influence

	WT × V = S	Factor

Overall economic conditions
Employment trends
Job market information

Total: _____ Economic influence

	WT × V = S	Factor

Perceived effect of race, sex, or
   ethnic background on success
Perceived effect of physical or
   psychological disabilities on success

Total: _____ Societal influence

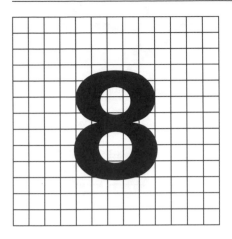

CAREERS IN HUMAN RESOURCE MANAGEMENT

CHAPTER OBJECTIVES

Upon completion of this chapter, you should be able to:

1. Describe the work of human resource management specialists.
2. Discuss current trends in human resource management and their impact on careers.
3. Diagram career paths for workers in human resource management.
4. Discuss job opportunities in the field of human resource management.
5. List the educational preparation and skills needed for entry and advancement in human resource management careers.
6. Evaluate careers in human resource management according to your individualized career decision-making model.

In the past, annual reports always have focused on the physical and financial assets of an organization. Today, more than ever before, *people* are an organization's most valuable resource for working toward organizational goals. The shrinking work force, the demand for workers with the requisite technological skills, and the shift to a service-oriented economy have caused organizations to place greater emphasis on qualified people and value human resources more highly. Consequently, more importance also is being placed on the human resource professionals whose job is the selection, training, development, servicing, and evaluation of employees. Formerly called personnel management, the term *human resource management* has come into existence to better reflect the increasing scope and importance of this crucial function in an organization.

The importance of human resources should be evident if you review the previous chapters, which address the changes in jobs and functions as a result of technology, mergers, global economics, or demand for better-quality products and services. The financial impact of these changes is great. One large organization calculated that it would incur a single loss of $55,000 if the wrong manager were recruited, hired, and trained for a position and then left before becoming a productive employee. Training and developing employees is a $30-billion function. Attracting and rewarding productive employees is accomplished in part by offering the best benefits packages, which may add 50 percent to the value of an individual's income. Other financial factors affecting organizations and employees are related to life-style issues such as relocation, health, and career growth.

Human resource management is a field for those who enjoy working with people and are good at it. Within this field are well-defined functional areas. These areas and the jobs associated with them afford many career options. This chapter will cover these options and includes such information as:

- what type of work is done in the area of human resource management
- where human resource management specialists are employed
- salaries and career paths
- latest trends
- job opportunities
- education and skills needed to pursue careers in human resource management
- sources of additional information

THE JOB

The top position, *director of human resource management*, is a demanding one. One aspect of the director's job is holding conferences with managers of other departments to ascertain future personnel needs, to define training and development needs, to develop and implement performance appraisal programs, and to suggest guidelines for promotion and firing. Within the department of human resource management, the director establishes departmental procedures, organizes the areas of work, supervises subordinates, and personally handles administrative details in hiring executive personnel. The director usually is active in professional organizations and keeps up with current trends in all areas of human resource management. Human resource managers can rise through the ranks as generalists or as specialists in one of the following areas.

Employment and placement. An area involving numerous jobs and a variety of duties is employment and placement. The *employment manager* has overall responsibility for the selection of qualified employees who have growth potential. Working under the manager are the *employment interviewers*, who evaluate applicants on the basis of personal interviews, and the *test administrators*, who conduct and score tests designed to measure an applicant's competence to do the job. Test administrators also may coordinate assessment centers in which employees are given various performance-based activities to determine their qualifications for specific positions. Often *college recruiters* conduct on-campus interviews to identify prospects for employment. Once an individual is hired, an *employee orientation specialist* provides the individual with information needed for smooth integration into company life.

In addition, the employment and placement professionals work with the manager to develop sources of potential employees to fill current and future human resource needs, to counsel employees should job-related problems or needs arise, and to administer the promotion and transfer system within the company. They also may provide outplacement activities, such as job counseling and resume preparation, should an employee be dismissed or laid off.

Training and career development. Under the guidance of the *training and development director*, a staff of *training and career specialists* develop and conduct programs to meet specific training needs; administer on-the-job training programs; maintain records of employee participation in training, such as management development, apprenticeship, career, and skills development programs; coordinate employee appraisal programs; and communicate to employees through company publications information and opportunities that may contribute to their professional growth and career development. Training and career specialists have a wide array of information and training technology at their disposal for their training programs. They can hire speakers and consultants to come into the company to conduct training sessions. In addition to in-house training and development, training and career specialists may coordinate company-paid educational opportunities for individual employees at local colleges and universities.

Wage and salary administration. The *wage and salary administrator* works to establish policies and practices that assure employees equitable pay. The administrator is assisted by the *job analyst*, who examines and interprets job duties, writes job descriptions, and assists in developing job specifications or responsibility areas. Jobs are evaluated by a *wage and salary specialist* to determine their proper pay range. An aspect of the wage and salary administrator's job is conducting compensation surveys to see how competitive the company's pay range is with similar jobs in other companies. This function will become increasingly important as the labor pool shrinks and the competition among companies for qualified workers heats up.

Benefits, services, and safety. This area includes a variety of activities involving programs for employees. The *benefits coordinator* develops and administers the organization's medical, disability, stock ownership, retirement, and pension plans. The *benefits planning analyst* may research new benefits options for the organization as well as review competing organizations' compensation packages.

The *employee relations director*, along with the *employee relations specialists*, coordinate and offer a wide range of services to employees. Services and programs may deal with issues such as alcohol and drug abuse treatment; dual-career couples; problems, such as maternity leave for parents and availability of child-care centers; relocation assistance; coping strategies to handle stress from both job and personal problems; and recreation, health, and fitness opportunities. Companies are finding that healthy employees are more productive. Today, numerous companies provide on-site fitness centers where employees can work out during lunch breaks. Many companies sponsor teams of employees who compete against teams from other companies in various athletic events. Company-sponsored recreational events to foster good employee relations and high morale are becoming more and more common.

The objective of employee relations is to take a positive and active approach to retaining employees and improving their productivity. Employee relations specialists must monitor changing life-style preferences and needs of employees to develop programs and services consistent with them.

The *safety director*, with the assistance of *plant safety specialists*, works with management in developing and administering safety programs. This team of safety specialists conducts safety inspections, maintains accident records, and submits required governmental health and safety reports. This job has become more complicated as new regulations have been added and old ones changed.

Industrial relations.   The position of *industrial relations director* is an important one in large companies today. The industrial relations director and staff of *industrial relations representatives* reflect the position of the company in transactions with union officials and employee union members. Involved in this job are such duties as negotiating labor contracts with union representatives, interpreting labor contracts to supervisors, resolving employee grievances, and collecting and analyzing information related to labor contracts.

Equal employment opportunity/affirmative action.   The coordination of management attempts to comply with equal opportunity and affirmative action laws and regulations is the responsibility of the *equal employment opportunity coordinator*. Aided by *equal employment opportunity specialists*, the coordinator performs such duties as writing the organization's affirmative action plan, assisting managers in developing affirmative action programs, advising management of legal requirements, investigating employee complaints and charges of discrimination, serving as liaison with minority and women's organizations, and representing the company in government investigations.

CAREER PATHS AND COMPENSATION

In human resource management, jobs have fairly specific duties. However, well-trained individuals can handle a number of positions seen in Figure 8-1. With experience come increased salary and advancement into one of the key positions that report to the director of human resource management. Salary is dependent upon company size, location, and a number of other factors. For example, a company with a complicated

Figure 8-1 Human resource management positions, salaries, and mobility

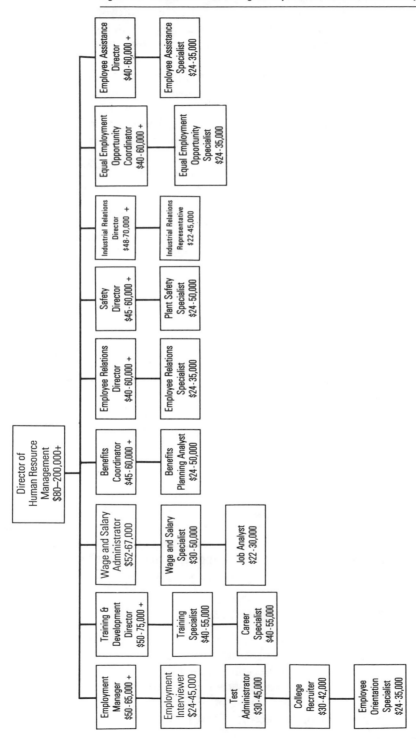

labor-management situation might pay well over $70,000 a year for a highly qualified labor relations director. Or, a company investing a sizable amount of money in training programs will want the best training director on the market and be willing to pay top dollar for the right individual.

The increased importance of the human resource management field has resulted in above-average increases in salary over the past several years. According to the March 1991 issue of the *College Placement Council Salary Survey*, new bachelor's degree candidates received offers averaging $22,429 a year for human resources/industrial relations positions. Beginners can start for as much as $28,000 a year and earn around $58,000 annually at midcareer. The average total compensation, including bonuses, for the director of human resources ranges from $90,000 in small to medium-sized firms to $150,000 in large companies. This figure can be as high as $200,000 for some directors.

"The Twelfth Annual *Working Woman* Salary Survey" that appeared in the January 1991 issue of *Working Woman* cites the Bureau of Labor Statistics figure that overall, women still earn only 70 cents to men's dollar for equal work. The greatest salary discrimination was found in human resource/personnel management—where, ironically, wage setting takes place. Female personnel and industrial relations managers averaged only 57 percent of the salaries of male colleagues in 1989.

In the past, individuals advancing through the personnel ranks have had little opportunity to advance to the chief executive position and have not had the level of influence in the organization that managers of other functional areas have had. The expanding role of human resource management has changed the outlook for advancement to some extent, particularly in services industries.

CURRENT TRENDS

The wave of acquisitions, mergers, divestitures, and bankruptcies that occurred throughout the 1980s resulted in a rash of corporate restructuring and layoffs. The responsibility of handling the employee upheaval was left to human resource professionals. Processing and keeping records was facilitated through the new technologies affecting all areas of business today. Human Resource Information Systems provides computer assistance in calculating and storing figures required for payroll and for compliance with government requirements. Maintaining accurate records of hirings, firings, and layoffs, especially in periods of large employee turnover, also is helped by computer applications. An important function of these systems is to provide timely information for management decision making.

Technology also has had a great impact on the topic of training. Continuing education now is required for all technical employees. Both computer-assisted instruction and computer-based training programs are increasing. Because of the costs of such programs, more organizations have begun to rely on external consultants and specialists. Consultants offer every kind of training and packaged program from human relations skills to motivation.

Organizations facing change now or in the future need employees who are skilled and able to meet new responsibilities. Training is not limited to new or lower-level employees. Executive management development requires creative and challenging programs. Management development series and programs are seen on public broadcasting stations. *Quality circles* engage employees at all levels in problem-solving and productivity sessions.

Managers who are dismissed as a result of restructuring often receive assistance in finding new positions through the outplacement efforts of employment and career development specialists. This service, along with wellness programs and the others mentioned earlier, is becoming more frequent as companies begin to accept more responsibility for the well-being of their employees.

Catalyst, a not-for-profit organization, works with corporations and individuals to develop career and family options. Catalyst has developed materials to help college students explore these options prior to joining organizations. The new computer-assisted career guidance systems, such as DISCOVER FOR ORGANIZATIONS and SIGI PLUS, deal with adult issues such as making transitions, changing careers, acquiring additional training, and managing time. Other career development programs continue to expand as individuals and organizations identify their needs and options for the future.

JOB OPPORTUNITIES

Workers in the field of human resource management are employed throughout the private and public sectors and in every industry. Nine out of ten are employed in private industry by manufacturers, banks, insurance companies, airlines, retail outlets, and other businesses. Some personnel professionals are employed in private employment agencies, executive search firms, professional recruiting organizations and temporary job placement services—the most rapidly growing segment of the job placement industry. Other human resource specialists find positions with local, state, and federal government. Opportunities will be excellent in state and local government. Special knowledge of government regulations is a major selling feature for job candidates. Industrial relations specialists are employed by labor unions as well as by private industry and government.

Demand   Personnel, training, and industrial relations specialists and managers held about 422,000 jobs in 1988, according to the Bureau of Labor Statistics. Of these positions, 252,000 were held by specialists and the rest were managers. The projection is for faster-than-average growth through the year 2000. The most rapid employment growth is expected in management, consulting, and job placement firms or agencies.

Employment interviewers will be in especially great demand, increasing in number by 33,000 (40 percent) between 1988 and 2000. Continued growth in the areas of employee benefits and services and safety programs will create jobs. Training and development specialists will be required in greater numbers. The need for specialized training and retraining of employees is largely due to more complex jobs, declining productivity, an aging work force with obsolete skills, and a technology explosion that employers must take advantage of in order to remain competitive. Although an increase of 91,000 jobs (22 percent) from 1988 to the year 2000 for human resource specialists and managers is predicted, the substantial pool of recent college graduates and qualified experienced workers will keep the job market in human resource management competitive.

Equal Opportunity Standing

Women have always done well in human resource management. Many women are promoted into human resource management from clerical positions. This may explain in part the salary discrimination. More women managers are employed in human resource management than in other areas. In addition, women own a number of employment agencies.

APTITUDES AND ATTRIBUTES NEEDED FOR SUCCESS

Education

Although many people have worked into human resource management positions from clerical positions in the past, the competitive job market now makes it more difficult to do this. In most organizations an undergraduate degree, preferably in business, is required for entry-level positions and absolutely essential for advancement. Past studies indicate that roughly 40 percent of human resource management professionals have at least a master's degree.

A broad knowledge of business and a familiarity with social sciences is the best background for work in human resource management. An undergraduate management degree with a major in personnel or industrial relations—coupled with courses in psychology, sociology, economics, political science, and written and oral communications—is good educational preparation for human resource management. A proficiency with computers and some knowledge of human resource information systems is becoming more important every day.

Certain areas require specialized knowledge. For example, human resource specialists interested in training and development should have some knowledge of teaching techniques, and those interested in industrial relations should have some knowledge of business law regarding labor unions.

Accreditation

Human resource management professionals can become accredited at a basic or senior level. At the senior level, options exist for accreditation as a generalist or as a specialist in one of six human resource management functions.

Personal Characteristics

Certain personal characteristics are necessary for success in human resource management careers. These include an ability to communicate at any level with all types of people. Flexibility, maturity, persuasiveness, good judgment, leadership, analytical ability, and the ability to handle pressure and sensitive situations calmly are vital to human resource management work.

SOURCES OF ADDITIONAL INFORMATION

If you are interested in human resource management, you can gain much insight into the field by reading such professional journals as *Human Resource Magazine*, *Personnel Journal*, and *Personnel Management*. In addition, the professional associations listed herein are excellent sources of information.

Society for Human Resource
  Management
606 N. Washington Street
Alexandria, VA 22314

American Society for Training
  and Development
1630 Duke Street
Box 1443
Alexandria, VA 22313

International Association for
  Personnel Women
194-A Harvard Street
Medford, MA 02155

Association for Quality and
  Participation
801-B W. Eighth Street, Suite 501
Cincinnati, OH 45203

International Personnel
  Management Association
1617 Duke Street
Alexandria, VA 22314

National Association of
  Personnel Consultants
3133 Mt. Vernon Avenue
Alexandria, VA 22305

National Council for Labor
  Reform
406 S. Plymouth Court
Chicago, IL 60605

For information on accreditation, write:

Personnel Accreditation Institute
c/o Society for Human Resource
  Management
606 N. Washington Street
Alexandria, VA 22314

For more information on Catalyst and its programs for organizations and individuals, write:

Catalyst
250 Park Avenue South
New York, NY 10003

CAREER DECISION-MAKING MODEL

The careers in this chapter offer still more possibilities for you to consider. Use the career decision-making model to help determine whether a career in human resources management is a likely alternative for you. Figure 8-2 is a form with the factors included from the career decision-making model described in detail in Chapter 1. Follow these directions in completing it.

1. Enter the position that interests you most on the line entitled *Job*.
2. Enter any additional factors used to personalize your model (from Chapter 1) in the blank spaces provided.
3. Enter the weights that you assigned to the factors (from Chapter 1) in the column *WT*. (It would be wise to review the explanations of the factors in the description of the model in Chapter 1 before going on to Step 4).
4. Assign a value from 1 (lowest) to 10 (highest) to each factor based on the information in this chapter and on your personal self-assessment, entering the value in the column *V*. If you feel that you have a certain aptitude or attribute needed for success in this career area, you should assign a fairly high value. If a certain interest, such as amount of variety, is important to you and you feel the area provides the variety you enjoy, assign a fairly high value. If not, assign a low value. Use this technique to assign values to all factors in the model. If you cannot assign a value based on the information in the chapter for some of the factors in the model, either use other sources to acquire the information or leave the space beside the factor blank.
5. Multiply the weight times the value, entering the score in the column *S*.

6. Add the scores in column S for each group of factors, entering the number in the space labeled *Total*.

You will use this evaluation in Chapter 11 in combination with evaluations of each career explored in this book.

WHAT DID YOU LEARN?

This chapter described careers in human resource management. You learned about the nature of the work, salary, career path information, current trends, the job outlook, education and skills needed for success, and where to obtain additional information. You completed a career evaluation for human resource management.

Although many specific managerial positions have been discussed throughout this book, you will gain real insight into management and supervision by reading the next chapter. Chapter 9, Careers in Management and Supervision, is devoted entirely to a discussion of the challenges and headaches of the much-sought-after leadership positions.

Figure 8-2 Career evaluation for human resource management

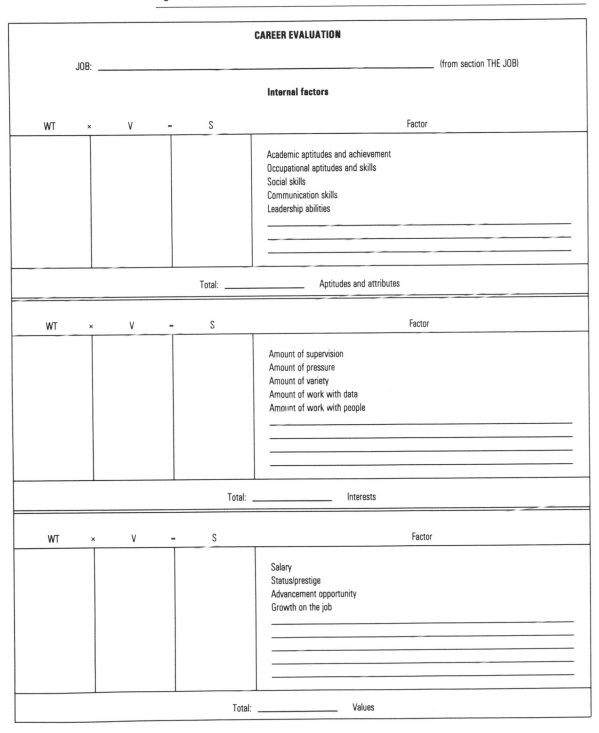

CAREER EVALUATION

JOB: _____ (from section THE JOB)

Internal factors

WT	×	V	=	S	Factor
					Academic aptitudes and achievement
					Occupational aptitudes and skills
					Social skills
					Communication skills
					Leadership abilities

Total: _____ Aptitudes and attributes

WT	×	V	=	S	Factor
					Amount of supervision
					Amount of pressure
					Amount of variety
					Amount of work with data
					Amount of work with people

Total: _____ Interests

WT	×	V	=	S	Factor
					Salary
					Status/prestige
					Advancement opportunity
					Growth on the job

Total: _____ Values

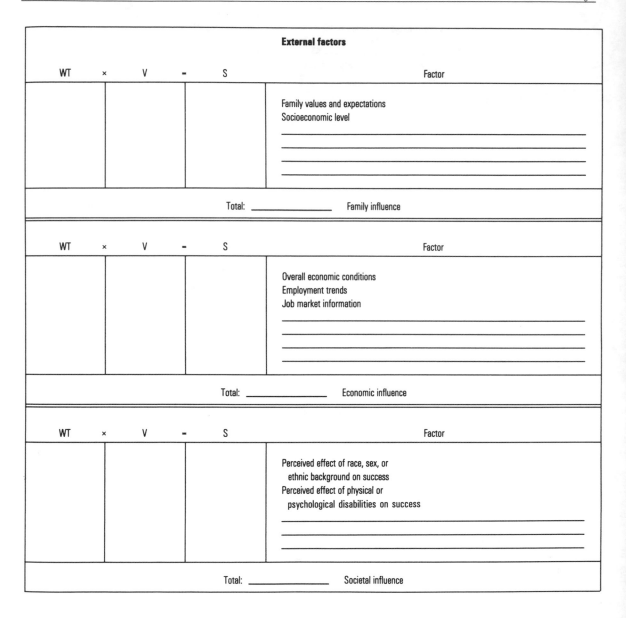

External factors

WT	×	V	-	S		Factor
						Family values and expectations
						Socioeconomic level

Total: _____ Family influence

WT	×	V	-	S		Factor
						Overall economic conditions
						Employment trends
						Job market information

Total: _____ Economic influence

WT	×	V	-	S		Factor
						Perceived effect of race, sex, or
						ethnic background on success
						Perceived effect of physical or
						psychological disabilities on success

Total: _____ Societal influence

CAREERS IN MANAGEMENT AND SUPERVISION

CHAPTER OBJECTIVES

Upon completion of this chapter, you will be able to:

1. Describe the work of managers and supervisors.
2. Discuss trends in management and their impact on careers.
3. Explain career paths in relation to management levels.
4. Discuss job opportunities in management and supervision.
5. List the educational preparation and skills needed for success in management and supervision.
6. Evaluate careers in management and supervision according to your individualized career decision-making model.

One of the most varied and widespread career areas in business is management and supervision. Managers and supervisors already have been discussed to some extent throughout this book. Managerial and supervisory positions are incorporated into a discussion of every career path. As you have learned already, not all individuals aspire to management positions. However, attached to positions in management are often increased status, higher salaries, and authority. The amount of authority depends on how high up an individual is in the management ranks. Still, speaking collectively, managers in both the private and public sectors run this country and in their hands rest the economic and social well-being of the public.

Corporations of today have streamlined management considerably. In the 1970s, it was customary to have as many as 12 to 15 levels of supervision in large corporations. In the 1990s, 5 or 6 levels is the norm. This streamlining is the result of major restructuring brought about by a wave of acquisitions and divestitures, increased global competition, an attempt at creating a more entrepreneurial environment to foster new product development, and a recessionary economy. The reduction of middle-level managers has increased both the complexity and the pressures of management positions.

This chapter will discuss the careers of managers and supervisors. The discussion will be general rather than specific. Information will include:

- what activities managers and supervisors perform
- career paths
- latest trends
- job opportunities
- education and skills needed to pursue management and supervisory careers
- sources of additional information

THE JOB

To say that the work of managers today is complex is to grossly under-state the situation. The organization exists as part of a larger system, and managers are concerned not only with employees and customers, but also with the social, political, economic, and technological influence of the greater environment in which the organization operates.

The key task of managers is to make decisions in light of the con-founding information and restrictions that come from politicians, econ-omists, labor leaders, environmentalists, scientists, engineers, consumers, and, in fact, society as a whole. Yet, they are the decision makers who influence the lives and directions of all these groups.

So who would want such a job? The answer is, many people—and competition for management positions permeates the organization at all levels. Many seek the higher status, greater salaries, and authority, but usually there is much more to it. Many employees have a strong sense of commitment to their organizations and want to contribute to the positive change or growth that takes place within them. Others want to utilize their full potential. Survival of an organization depends on the ability of its managers to cope with change and renew the organization so that it remains strong and healthy.

Management Functions

Although each managerial position in every organization is unique in terms of the specific activities in which the manager is involved, gener-ally managers perform the same four major functions: planning, orga-nizing, directing, and controlling.

Planning   involves establishing goals, defining objectives, and develop-ing long- and short-term strategies for accomplishing these objectives. Planning is becoming more and more important; it assures that an orga-nization will survive the present to have a future. Using numerous mana-gerial tools to forecast future developments in the economy, the industry, and the company is essential to the planning process.

Organizing   involves establishing a structure that enables individuals to work together productively. The establishment of departments, the de-sign of jobs, the assignment of responsibility, and the delegation of au-thority are all part of it.

Directing or administering   involves setting up the guidelines and con-ditions for employees under which they may perform the jobs that en-able the organization to reach its goals. Good working conditions, fair compensation, proper motivation, effective communication, good train-ing, and counseling are all part of directing.

Controlling provides for the feedback of information to management about how well actual performance measures up to planned objectives. Suppose production were lower than management expected. The reasons would be determined and either strategies for improving production would be developed or the objective would be changed. This is part of the controlling process.

Many quantitative tools used in planning and controlling are developed and taught in the branch of management study called *management science*. Other planning and controlling techniques as well as techniques for organizing and directing are developed and taught in the branch of management study called *organizational theory and behavior*.

Other activities that managers perform in conjunction with the four major functions are making decisions, communicating critical information, allocating resources, and managing conflict and change.

Supervision

Supervision is an aspect of management. Supervisors oversee the work being done by subordinates. They are involved in maintaining a healthy work environment, motivating employees to do their best, conducting on-the-job training, assisting subordinates with both work and personal problems, communicating organizational policies and procedures, evaluating individual performance, and providing input to managers helpful in decision making.

All managers are supervisors, but *not all supervisors are managers*. This may seem like a paradox, but it really isn't. Managers delegate some of their directing responsibilities to supervisors so that they can devote more time to the other managerial functions. Supervisors usually do not make major strategic planning or organizational decisions. Supervisors follow guidelines that have been developed by managers. Some eventually move into management positions; others do not. This distinction will be discussed more fully in the section on career paths.

Line and staff

Managers can occupy either line or staff positions. The *line* position performs the direct tasks necessary to fulfill the functions of a specific department, for example, production. The *staff* position performs the indirect tasks necessary to support the line position, for example, computer support to the production department. Whether the position is a line or staff position depends on the structure of the organization. A marketing department in one organization may use telecommunications to link its regional and national sales personnel. A marketing department of another organization may use telecommunications in direct sales campaigns, thus more directly in selling the product. The telecommunications manager in the first organization is in a staff position, while the manager in the second organization is in a line position. The implications of occupying line or staff positions will be discussed in the section on career paths.

Specialization

Management is management! But, from the kinds of management positions already discussed in previous chapters of this book, it can be seen that a level of technical competence or an area of specialization is very important for breaking into management. Obviously, the information processing manager must have some knowledge of computers and information technology; the advertising manager, of advertising, and so on. In certain industries, for instance chemicals or electronics, an aspiring manager would need advanced technical knowledge in these areas. Often, the technical competence is gained in an undergraduate degree program and the management skills are acquired through management training and development programs or an MBA program.

Some specialty areas in management have become fields in themselves. These include hotel and restaurant management, hospital administration, airport management, and city management. Undergraduate and, in some cases, graduate programs are available to those interested in managing hotels, restaurants, hospitals, airports, and cities. These programs provide the special knowledge required for these unique management assignments.

It is impossible to explore in depth the many management possibilities in a single chapter or even in an entire book. But at this point a base of general knowledge of what management is all about has been laid. This knowledge will be refined even more in the following discussion of career paths.

CAREER PATHS AND COMPENSATION

There are various degrees of authority in management. It is the degree of authority granted an individual that denotes management rank. Major levels of management are diagrammed in Figure 9-1. In large companies, there are dozens of ranks within each level. Speaking generally, supervisors often are considered first-level management; department managers and general managers, which include regional and plant managers, are labeled middle management; and vice-presidents and chief executives are top management or executives.

As a manager moves up the ranks, some changes in emphasis on certain managerial competencies take place. First-level management positions require that a high level of technical competence be exhibited by the manager. This is because of the role of first-level managers in training workers to perform technical tasks and overseeing the work to be sure that the tasks performed are up to the standard. In a first-level management position, one is rarely called upon to demonstrate a conceptual competence or the ability to see the "big picture." However, promotion

Figure 9-1 Levels of management

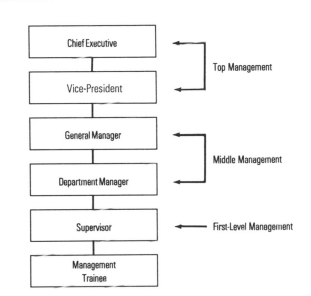

may well depend on an individual's potential to do this. The middle manager must demonstrate both technical and conceptual competence. At the executive levels, managers rarely have occasion to demonstrate their technical competence but rather spend the majority of their time dealing with the large conceptual issues of the organization. The executive in the large organization is remote from many of the interpersonal aspects and works with only a few key executives. The job is less spectacular and more impersonal than many would expect. A significant amount of effort of top management is directed toward establishing a philosophy and code of ethics under which the firm will operate to fulfill its complex responsibility to its stockholders, employees, customers, and the public.

Throughout first, middle, and top levels of management, managerial competence is needed uniformly to perform the key management functions. A first-level manager displaying high technical and managerial competence will be promoted to middle management. A demonstration of conceptual competence by the middle manager may give that individual a good shot at a key executive position.

Trainees. Often management trainees begin in supervisory positions or are trained by supervisors. If their performance is impressive, they advance to management positions. In some cases, a position as supervisor is at the top of an individual's career path because of limited skills or educational background. When this occurs, the supervisor frequently trains those who do move into management. Although this is often not an easy situation for supervisors who have come up through the worker ranks, have demonstrated their commitment to the organization, and are considerably older than the management trainees, still this is the situation that prevails in many organizations.

Advancement

It is not only lack of education or personal leadership attributes that might hinder an individual's advancement up through the management ranks. Recall the discussion in Chapter 1 about the entry-level position. Remember that from the time an individual enters a company, no matter how unnoticed that individual might feel, someone *is* noticing. Such things matter as the attitude and enthusiasm with which an individual does his or her *own* job and the quality of the work performed. No one ever gets promoted by doing someone else's job. Patience and tenacity are very important. Today companies need potential managerial talent as much as management trainees hope to enter the ranks. Do a good job and usually it will be recognized. Although patience is an important virtue in overly enthusiastic beginners, don't be too patient. If a beginner does not make an upward move after a couple of years, he or she can either settle in and work toward retirement or change companies.

Line vs. staff.   Whether one chooses a line or staff position also may be important. Most career paths diagrammed in the previous chapters show line paths. Advancement is usually from entry-level to top line-management positions within the career fields. However, as discussed earlier, organizations may differ somewhat on whether a department or position is considered line or staff. Recall the example of the telecommunications managers. While both may report to the marketing director, future advancement will depend upon the individual's ability to manage the entire marketing department, coordinate with directors who are at similar levels, and interact with the manager at the next level up.

Organizational structure.   A critical aspect of upward mobility in management is an understanding of the structure of the particular organization in which an individual works and which positions are fast-track—that is, highly promotable—and which are dead-end. An individual should diagram a desired career path within an organization and a time frame for moving from one position to another. The path should be based on previous patterns of mobility from one position to another within the company. For example, once an individual enters an organization, he or she should choose a top position for which to shoot, and working downward determine all previous positions held by the person currently in that position as well as the background and qualifications of those currently holding each of the positions. Young aspirants should try to avoid having a superior who is not promotable and, if unavoidably assigned to such an individual, should attempt to transfer as soon as possible.

Mentors. The single most important action that a new employee takes is finding a mentor. A mentor is an older professional in the same field, preferably someone making steady career progress up the company ladder. Good mentors offer introductions to people higher up and a good many insights into the unspoken rules in the company. Every company has a unique corporate culture and its own way of doing things.

Finding a mentor is not easy. Any mentor worth having is extremely busy and not out looking for protégés. The young employee who shows persistence yet flexibility, works hard to obtain recognition, listens to everything going on in the company before taking strong positions or forming alliances, has clearly stated career goals, and displays confidence and pride as well as ability will attract attention before long. Many employees have followed their mentors along the hierarchy by filling the positions they vacate on the way up.

It is particularly important for women to have mentors, for women are greatly underrepresented in middle and top levels of management in larger companies. Women's salaries lag behind those of men for the same positions. A recent *Business Week* Harris poll reported that 60 percent of women in management in large corporations identified "a male-dominated corporate culture" as an obstacle to success. Some companies, however, make a concerted effort to remove obstacles preventing women's advancement into corporate management ranks through programs such as awareness training for men. Some companies even set goals for promoting women.

Women in management. The August 6, 1990, issue of *Business Week* reported results of a study conducted to identify companies with "women-friendly" corporate cultures. The factors considered were numbers of women in key executive positions and on the board of directors, specific efforts to help women advance, and sensitivity to the work/family dilemma. The following six companies rated very highly: Avon, CBS, Dayton-Hudson, Gannett, Kelly Services, and U.S. West. Not surprisingly, two of these companies are in women-intensive industries. The next group of companies had made "substantial progress" in advancing women. It included American Express, Baxter International, Corning, Honeywell, IBM, Johnson & Johnson, Merck, Monsanto, Pitney Bowes, Reader's Digest, and Security Pacific Bank. These companies covered a wide variety of industries. Women have fared very well in computer companies, the study reported, entering in substantial numbers when their skills were much-needed at the birth of the industry. But other industries represented in the study were old, conservative industries such as banking and electrical manufacturing. The companies represented bucked usual practices to become women-friendly. Honorable mentions went to Digital Equipment, DuPont, Hewlett-Packard, Olin, 3M, and Xerox.

Though women have had to work hard to prove themselves, every successful woman changes a few minds. Women's networks in companies often help other women learn the ropes. It is important for young women aspiring to management positions to be aware of how women are faring at the companies that are making them offers. Questions to ask at interviews should include: What percentage of women hold top management posts? Middle management posts? Do company benefits include extended leaves, flex time, day-care assistance? The best offer for a new graduate may not come from a reputedly women-friendly company, but from a company simply offering excellent training and development opportunities. Trade offs are always present in job offers. It is important for both men and women to carefully articulate their short- and long-range goals before entering the job market.

Salaries

The most upwardly mobile positions do not always offer the highest salaries. Don't get sidetracked by dollar signs and end a budding career! Individuals who do their organizational homework when first entering a company will get the picture fairly quickly and make intelligent career decisions. To assure that individuals have lots of choices, they should promote themselves throughout the organization. Movement among various departments helps a manager develop an appreciation for the overall operation, which is excellent grooming for an executive slot.

A discussion of average earnings or range of earnings of managers collectively would be more misleading than helpful. Salary figures in earlier chapters give some idea of what professional managers earn. Even those salaries were qualified in terms of the size of the firm, the employing industry, and the level of authority. Managers do not always earn more for the authority and responsibility they assume. In some areas of sales, individuals might experience a reduction in salary upon movement into management. Sometimes workers who are highly skilled in advanced technological areas, such as physics or engineering, may earn higher salaries than the manager under whom they work. Certainly doctors earn substantially more than hospital administrators in most cases. So, although most managers do fairly well in terms of salary, many outside of management do as well or better. Salary, as stressed earlier, is only part of a career decision and, in the area of management, is a somewhat ambiguous matter as it is.

If salary level is of primary importance at a given point in your career, you will want to investigate specific conditions and salaries in related jobs at that time, and make your career moves based on current and potential salaries and other incomes, such as benefits and commissions.

CURRENT TRENDS

Organizational Structure   The complex social, political, and environmental conditions today have brought about changes in management careers and, indeed, even in the structure of organizations. The 1980s were characterized by thousands of mergers, acquisitions, and divestitures. As companies and pieces of companies were bought and sold, hundreds of thousands of managers and professionals were forced to change jobs or retire early. In many cases, middle-level management positions were never refilled. Major reorganizations took place. Top management realized that if the firm was to compete in a more competitive, rapidly changing business environment, it had to respond more rapidly to change. Though reducing costs in increasingly tight economic conditions was a factor in not replacing many middle-level managers, an even more important factor was introducing products into the market more efficiently.

For years, primarily small companies have been credited with introducing new technology into the marketplace. One of the reasons for this is the efficiency of less-formal corporate structure in a smaller firm. While new products were still being discussed as possibilities through fifteen levels of management in large companies, small companies functioning as entrepreneurial teams had moved a product from the drawing board to the marketplace. The message was clear—until large corporations began to be more entrepreneurial both in philosophy and in practice, they would be unable to beat their small competitors into the marketplace with new, technology-oriented products.

So big companies responded to the challenge. As a result of reorganization within these companies, more project or product development teams emerged. These teams were given the authority to operate fairly autonomously both in fulfilling goals and in competing for company resources. Product managers reported directly to top management. Because the teams were entrepreneurial in spirit, yet part of a large corporation, the term intrepreneuring was coined.

Organizational structures are beginning to depart from the standard pyramid structure, with its well-developed level of middle management, and move in the direction of top-management teams. The idea is that the group's synergy will produce better solutions to the extremely complicated problems facing top management today. These teams, with the use of computer technology and sophisticated mathematical tools, can make timely decisions and pass them directly to first-level managers, eliminating the necessity for a large number of middle-management positions.

In the absence of many levels of middle managers, managers operate their departments more autonomously and have more authority over both activities and budgets. Their offices usually are located close to top management, and communications are considerably less formal than in the huge bureaucracies of the past. Though chain of command is still intact in many organizations where managers at every level formally report

to a designated individual, communications are considerably more relaxed and pragmatic in most organizations.

Technology

Technology has changed corporate communications forever. Each manager has a personal computer, usually hooked into a central computer
through local area network (LAN) technology. Branch computers are
hooked into the central computer through wide area network (WAN)
technology. Thus, improved communications technology has enabled the
free flow of information throughout the organization.

Management information systems (MIS) and decision support systems (DSS) provide a systematic way of disseminating information
needed for management decisions. A *system* is a collection of people,
machines, programs, and procedures organized to perform a certain
task. Management information systems provide managers a steady
flow of timely, accurate information from a variety of resources, both
inside and outside the firm, that they then can use to make decisions.
In the past, many levels of management were necessary for organizing
and communicating this type of information alone. Today, improved
computer and communications technology has reduced this need
dramatically.

Also, computer technology and telecommunications networks allow
managers quicker access to needed information and assist in making
projections for various scenarios. In response, managers are expected to
make critical decisions in shorter periods of time. As a result, organizations themselves change more frequently, usually in structure and technology. Unless managers can effectively organize and implement the
changes, they may be replaced.

Many organizations are instituting management-succession plans to
insure that the organization will have competent individuals in key management positions. By identifying the crucial management positions
needed to fulfill organizational goals, top executives, along with human
resource managers, can identify the skills necessary to manage the functions. In turn, they can also identify individuals who either have the
skills now or can with training develop the skills for the future.

JOB OPPORTUNITIES

Demand

The future holds interesting prospects for young, ambitious beginners in
management. The Bureau of Labor Statistics predicts that the number of
managers will increase by 22 percent from 1988 to 2000, from 12.1 to 14.8
million. Of this increase, 479,000 (16 percent) will be in jobs for general
managers and top executives. Growth in management positions is attributed to more complex business operations and increasing employment in
trade and service areas. Specialized training and graduate study usually

are required. Also, the ability to use new information and communications technologies for managerial decision making is essential.

Supply

Currently, organizations are experiencing a decline in the numbers of potential executives in the age range of 50 to 65 years. Thus, experienced talent will be in short supply, and the available jobs will be filled with young, relatively inexperienced executives. Companies are expanding and refining their executive training programs in an effort to stay ahead of the game. Unless they do this, and quickly, there simply will be no one experienced and skillful enough to fill the anticipated vacancies.

Equal Opportunity Standing

Women are expected to fare better than in the past. By 1995, 60 percent of all workers will be female. Since many are already in the clerical and service industries, management positions for them should increase in the future. Computer technology has removed many of the physically demanding tasks of other kinds of work, thus increasing numbers of women in nontraditional occupations. In addition, more women are obtaining business degrees these days, as many as 50 percent in some schools. Of the 65,000 MBAs being granted, 30 percent are going to women.

Within organizations, special skill-building and career programs have been developed to help women advance. In addition, women have developed their own networks within organizations and within communities and professional organizations. For many career fields, women have formed their own professional organizations. Many of these organizations are listed at the ends of chapters in this book.

Women attempting to enter management probably have experienced at least as much sex bias as in any other area. The woman who is uninformed about the organizational hierarchy and has not done her organizational homework when first entering an organization may never even get close to the fast track. She will forever fall behind her male counterparts and never really understand why. There are a number of books and periodicals that are excellent reading for aspiring women managers. Two of the best magazines offering managerial career information are *Working Woman* and *Savvy*. As the saying goes, "Forewarned is forearmed." It is hoped that high demand for managers with executive potential coupled with management development programs will improve the picture somewhat for women.

APTITUDES AND ATTRIBUTES NEEDED FOR SUCCESS

More than 90 percent of business executives hold college degrees. A bachelor's degree is rapidly becoming necessary for entry into management, and graduate degrees are becoming common. Depending on the industry, a technical undergraduate degree in engineering, math, chemistry, or a liberal arts undergraduate degree are highly marketable *if* coupled with an MBA. The MBA is usually a generalist degree that gives an individual an overall understanding of business organizations and many of the tools and techniques of management. If four years is the limit you can afford to attend college, be aware that most companies prefer the business school graduates for management training.

There are a number of abilities essential to success in management. Included are:

- communications ability for reading, writing, speaking, and listening
- human relations ability for understanding and getting along with people
- management ability for analyzing problems, making decisions, and carrying out the basic management functions
- personal abilities such as judgment, personality, intuition, and self-confidence

SOURCES OF ADDITIONAL INFORMATION

There are a number of sources to which you can write for information on management careers. One of these, American Management Association, Inc., has prepared an excellent list of sources of information about careers which is available on request. For information, write:

American Management
 Association, Inc.
135 West 50th Street
New York, NY 10020

American Society for Public
 Administration
1120 G Street N.W., Suite 500
Washington, DC 20005

National Association for Female
 Executives
127 W. 24th Street
New York, NY 10011

National Management
 Association
2210 Arbor Boulevard
Dayton, OH 45439

Women in Management
Two North Riverside Plaza,
 Suite 2400
Chicago, IL 60606

CAREER DECISION-MAKING MODEL

Would you like to be a manager? Evaluate management as a career. Figure 9-2 is a form with the factors included from the career decision-making model described in detail in Chapter 1. Follow the directions on page 162 in completing it.

Figure 9-2 Career evaluation for management and supervision

CAREER EVALUATION

JOB: _____ (from section THE JOB)

Internal factors

WT	×	V	=	S	Factor
					Academic aptitudes and achievement
					Occupational aptitudes and skills
					Social skills
					Communication skills
					Leadership abilities
					_____
					_____
					_____

Total: _____ Aptitudes and attributes

WT	×	V	=	S	Factor
					Amount of supervision
					Amount of pressure
					Amount of variety
					Amount of work with data
					Amount of work with people
					_____
					_____
					_____

Total: _____ Interests

WT	×	V	=	S	Factor
					Salary
					Status/prestige
					Advancement opportunity
					Growth on the job
					_____
					_____
					_____
					_____

Total: _____ Values

Figure 9-2 Career evaluation for management and supervision (continued)

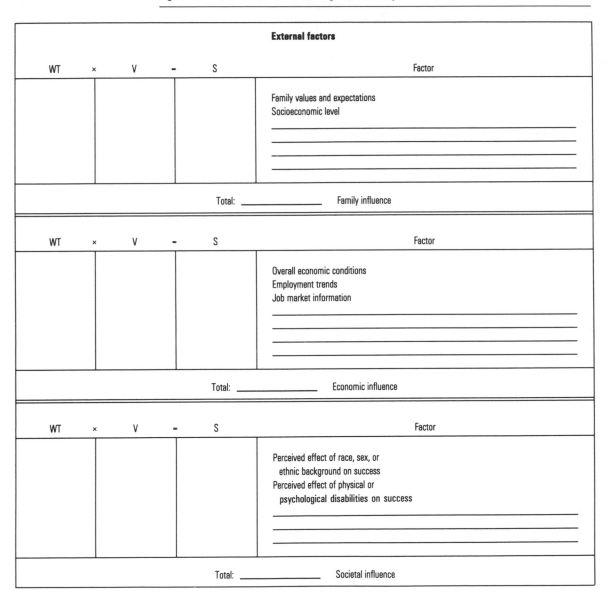

1. Enter the position that interests you most on the line titled *Job*.
2. Enter any additional factors used to personalize your model (from Chapter 1) in the blank spaces provided.
3. Enter the weights that you assigned to the factors (from Chapter 1) in the column *WT*. (It would be wise to review the explanations of the factors in the description of the model in Chapter 1 before going on to step 4.)

4. Assign a value from 1 (lowest) to 10 (highest) to each factor based on the information in this chapter and on your personal self-assessment, entering the value in the column V. If you feel that you have a certain aptitude or attribute needed for success in this career area, you should assign a fairly high value. If a certain interest, such as amount of variety, is desirable to you and you feel the area provides the variety you enjoy, assign a fairly high value. If not, assign a low value. Use this technique to assign values to all factors in the model. If you cannot assign a value based on the information in the chapter for some of the factors in the model, either use other sources to acquire the information or leave the space beside the factor blank.

5. Multiply the weight times the value and then enter the score in the column S.

6. Add the scores in column S for each group of factors entering the number in the space labeled *Total*.

You will use this evaluation in Chapter 11 in combination with evaluations of each career explored in this book.

WHAT DID YOU LEARN?

You have gained some very general knowledge of management and supervision which, when used in conjunction with the information provided in other chapters, should give you some ideas about your own future career path. An understanding of managerial functions and levels, career paths, trends, job opportunities, and education and skills needed for success in management is valuable in career planning. You completed a career evaluation for management and supervision.

To give you some interesting alternatives that might appeal to the independent-minded individual, Chapter 10 describes careers in business education, consulting, entrepreneurship, and franchising.

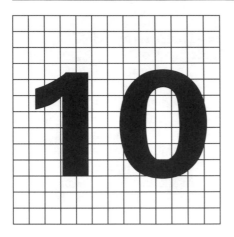

CAREERS IN BUSINESS, EDUCATION, CONSULTING, ENTREPRENEURSHIP, AND FRANCHISING

CHAPTER OBJECTIVES

Upon completion of this chapter, you should be able to:

1. Discuss the advantages and disadvantages of a career as a business educator, a consultant, and a business owner.
2. Describe the educational background, experience, and special abilities needed to be successful in business education, consulting, and business ownership.
3. Discuss the activities involved in owning and operating your own business.
4. Explain the pros and cons of franchise ownership.
5. Evaluate your interest in business education, consulting, and business ownership.

The 1980s and 1990s have been called the Era of the Entrepreneur. An entrepreneur is one who takes on the personal and financial risk of starting a business. Increases in new jobs in recent years are primarily due to the growth of small companies. New books and magazines cover the topic in great detail. Special features in established newspapers and magazines provide readers with how-to information and profiles of successful entrepreneurs and their businesses. Colleges and universities offer special classes and even degrees in entrepreneurship. Large organizations, recognizing the value of an entrepreneurial approach, look for employees who function as part of "entrepreneurial" teams to develop new products. Americans of all ages possess the entrepreneurial spirit. This spirit, in combination with knowledge and experience, contributes to success.

Challenging career options for business professionals also exist in the areas of education and consulting. These areas, along with business ownership, provide opportunities for people who value individuality, freedom, and variety. On the other hand, the work can be more demanding and require greater knowledge and skills than in other areas of business. For these reasons, the careers described in this chapter *may not be for beginners!*

The purpose of this chapter is to help you decide whether education, consulting, or business ownership are viable career options for you. You may decide that your interests are strong, but you lack some of the requirements for success at this time. In this case, any of these options can be incorporated into your career plan but as a medium- or long-range rather than an immediate goal. This chapter will make you aware of the challenges and risks involved in these careers and describe how to prepare yourself for entering these fields.

CAREERS IN BUSINESS EDUCATION

Professional business educators find teaching positions in two-and four-year colleges and universities offering programs in business. A master's degree in one of the business disciplines or an MBA is usually sufficient qualification for a teaching position in a community college. Depending on supply and demand, a doctorate might be required. It always helps to have the doctorate. A doctorate always is required for such tenure track positions as *professor* in four-year colleges and universities.

Educational Requirements

Earning one's doctorate requires a large commitment of both time and money. After a four-year bachelor's degree program, a master's program requiring at least two years of full-time study and usually a master's thesis must be undertaken. Successful completion of a master's-level program does not guarantee admission to a doctoral program. Applicants to graduate business programs must have earned a specified grade point average in undergraduate courses, obtained a certain score on the Graduate Management Admissions Test (GMAT), and demonstrated the potential for conducting original research. Doctoral programs require at least two years of full-time coursework and seminars along with the design and completion of a doctoral dissertation. This can be a lengthy process, depending on the design, and each step must be approved by a committee before the candidate may go on. Review of the literature, design of the project, data gathering or laboratory experimentation, and analysis of results can take well over a year to complete.

The reputation of the university and its doctoral program as well as the student's assigned major professor are factors that come into play when recent recipients of doctorates apply to prestigious and well-known universities. Therefore, those seeking doctorates should carefully evaluate a school and its program before entering. Finding a major professor who shares a student's research interests and who is well-known in the field can make doctoral study more valuable, and thus the student more marketable when entering the job market. Similar to the mentor in business organizations, the major professor can help the student develop the research interests and abilities to guarantee success in the academic community. At the same time, the student works hard for the major professor, enhancing that professor's productivity.

Job Opportunities

Demand. As the demand for business professionals increases, so increases the demand for educators. Demand may vary with the area of specialization. Professors in accounting, finance, and management information systems are in particular demand at this time. Doctoral candidates may concentrate in one or more specific areas within their chosen field—for example, accounting in not-for-profit businesses or marketing research in service industries. New doctorates are considered for positions as assistant professors. Selection criteria can include dissertation and other research publications, evaluations by professors, and experience outside the doctoral program, such as previous employment in business. In addition, teaching evaluations may be considered since most doctoral students teach undergraduate business classes as part of their graduate assistantships.

Positions. *Instructors* in two-year schools primarily teach but may be expected to write books and articles as well. University *professors* normally have lighter teaching loads but are required to publish articles in their field as a requirement for promotion and tenure. The "publish or perish" edict is in force in most colleges and universities. In addition, both instructors and professors are evaluated on service to their schools, which usually includes serving on committees and can involve fundraising. An assistant professor is promoted to associate professor, then full professor.

Often college professors enter administrative positions such as *department chair* or *dean*. Such posts as dean of undergraduate or graduate business studies or dean of the college of business administration are usually filled by former professors. Figure 10-1 shows the hierarchy of a typical university college of business. It is not unusual for professors to earn money outside the university as consultants and sometimes as entrepreneurs.

CAREERS IN CONSULTING

In good humor, consultants have been defined as professionals who have been out of work for more than two months. They borrow your watch, then tell you what time it is. Humor aside, consultants provide a valuable service in a constantly changing field. *Business consultants* are problem solvers with both extensive experience and an area of expertise. Specializing in various areas of business—such as strategic planning, information systems, feasibility studies, and market and product research—consultants are widely used throughout business and industry to help plan strategies and solve problems when strategies go awry. In 1988, there were more than 12,000 consulting firms and independent consultants in the United States and Canada. They are listed in the *Consultants and Consulting Organizations Directory* found in the reference section of many libraries.

Figure 10-1   University college of business hierarchy

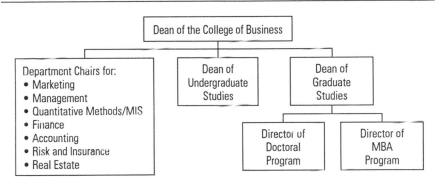

The Job

Since consultants work for many clients, they are exposed to different methods of solving problems and a variety of valuable sources of information. The consultant uses diverse experiences to analyze and solve problems for clients. Having a knowledge of what works and what doesn't in a variety of situations, the consultant makes recommendations that can save time and money. Most consultants have tremendous freedom over their time and other resources. Whether they free-lance, work in small companies, or work for large consulting firms, they work independently with individual clients. To be rehired for additional work by a client, a consultant must demonstrate the ability to help solve the client's problems in both creative and cost-effective ways. Consulting is not the job for someone who wants to work less and avoid the nine-to-five routine. Longer, though less routine, hours are required for successful consulting. Often client companies impose difficult-to-meet deadlines and expect unrealistic results. A consultant competes with other consultants for jobs.

Current Trends

The consulting industry has experienced double-digit growth over the past five years, but the rate of growth has begun to decline. While consultants are widely used, today they are facing a highly competitive market. This is primarily due to a recessionary environment when business practices are scaled down. Though the use of consultants may greatly benefit a business, they are not required for doing business and are one of the first budget items to be cut in hard times. Usually a low-profile industry, lately many consulting companies are increasing their efforts to actively market themselves.

According to a recent *Wall Street Journal* article, consulting companies previously having more work than they could handle now hire publicists, ask for and disseminate testimonials from clients, sponsor conferences, and advertise their services—sometimes on television. The following survey results indicate the percent of respondents using the listed promotional techniques to get clients:

Personal relationships/"old boy" network	60%
Participation in seminars	33
Mailing and phoning	13
Door-to-door selling	7
Advertising	3
Marketing agents	3
Public relations companies	3

These survey results demonstrate that a vital activity engaged in by consultants today is gaining clients.

Aptitudes and Attributes Needed for Success

Unless a company is rehiring a consultant who has worked for it previously, sometimes several consultants are scheduled for interviews. Who is hired depends on a number of things. The first is how well the interviewer and the consultant get along personally, since they usually will be working together. A second consideration is the quality of the consultant's references, including companies for which the consultant has completed an assignment similar to the one proposed. Though consultants may work for competing companies, often consulting contracts stipulate that the consultant may not disclose privileged company information or work for a competing firm for a certain time period. Finally, the number of years of experience and the quality of that experience are considered. Consulting fees vary greatly depending on the scope and complexity of the project and the reputation of the consultant. Well-established, successful consultants rarely lack employment. However, building a reputation as a consultant requires hard work over a number of years.

Job Opportunities

Consulting Firms. Since people are the greatest resource in consulting companies, everyone in large consulting companies gets involved in recruiting new employees. In general, consultants enter the field with two to four years of experience and a college degree, often an MBA or doctorate. Top consulting firms hire graduates from the best business schools, then train them. Summer internships are offered to promising candidates by these firms, enabling them to evaluate recruits performing typical tasks before offering them permanent employment with the firm.

Work in large consulting firms is characterized by pressure, long hours, travel, and high turnover. These firms are partnerships with an up-or-out policy—that is, consultants have from five to seven years to make partner. If they fail, they are out. Only one in five who begin work with a large company are expected to make partner. Many opt for consulting with large firms for the training and experience, then go out on their own by choice. Most consulting firms are based in the Northeast and in California. Larger firms have branches throughout the country.

Companies often use consultants on a continuing basis, so their work tends to be long-term oriented. Entry-level consulting work in large companies is primarily as a *researcher*. As *junior consultants* or *associates* demonstrate the analytic, interpersonal, and motivational skills required for success in the job, they are promoted to a position entitled *case team leader* or *senior consultant*. In this capacity, a consultant supervises a small team, normally working on one or two cases at a time. Three or four years later, if the senior consultant is performing well, he or she is promoted to *consulting manager*. As manager, a consultant leads a consulting team on important client projects. Once promoted to *junior partner* and finally *senior partner* or *director,* the consultant's work is primarily marketing the firm and its services. Figure 10-2 shows a career path in a large consulting firm.

Figure 10-2 Career path in a large consulting firm

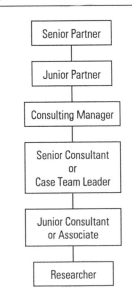

Though exceptional beginners may be hired out of college with under-graduate degrees, an MBA is required by most firms for advancement. Most beginners earn $28,000 to $34,000 a year with mid-year and end-of-year bonuses. College graduates with two years of experience can earn approximately $50,000 plus bonuses. MBAs earn salaries in the range of $45,000 to $90,000. Beginning consultants with MBAs from top business schools such as Harvard and Stanford earn $60,000 plus bonuses. Salaries increase dramatically with promotions. Junior partners earn in excess of $150,000 plus bonuses and shares in the firm. Senior partners earn within a range of from $300,000 to $600,000, with older seniors earning salaries in excess of $1 million.

Independent consulting   may be done on a full-time or part-time basis. Many university professors consult as a sideline to supplement their university salaries. Retired executives or executives between jobs find their experience and insights very marketable as consultants. A *strategic planning consultant* should have been employed as a successful manager in a position fairly high up in an organization before endeavoring to establish a reputation as a consultant. Although consultants are well-paid when they work, paying bills requires steady work. Self-employed consultants must earn 50 percent more money than consultants in firms to pay for the costs of doing business and the benefits normally provided by a company, such as health insurance, holidays and vacations, travel expenses, office space, supplies and equipment, clerical help, telephone expenses, and so on. The image projected through the consultant's dress, manners, and office will have great impact on landing jobs. Recall that when people pay a consultant considerably more than they pay the average manager, they expect a high degree of professionalism. Even though consultants are self-employed, they still are governed to some extent by the behavior and dress codes of the particular industry for which they consult. For example, consultants are better received in the banking and insurance industries if they are conservatively dressed. Men should be clean-shaven, and women should avoid heavy makeup. It is unlikely that one can be a "rugged individualist" and be a successful consultant at the same time.

An independent consultant has to be willing to hustle for jobs. One way to do this is to become known through publishing articles in trade journals. Still another way is to become actively involved in professional organizations, thus meeting many potential clients. Former clients also may help identify potential clients. Consultants must market their services by writing personal letters to executives who have the power to hire them. Consultants who want to run their consulting as a small business and maintain independent contractor status in the eyes of the Internal Revenue Service may use broker firms (who operate something like headhunters) to find consulting jobs. The broker earns from 25 to 40 percent of what the consultant is paid on the initial contact with the hiring company and less in subsequent contacts.

Independent consulting is not for everyone. But if you have expertise in a sought-after area of specialization; can sell yourself; are financially well-off enough to survive the lean times; and want the challenge and freedom of consulting—then go for it! Independent consultants who are unsuccessful can always give up the business and find a salaried job. Also,consultants may be employed by companies as internal consultants and have the challenge of a consulting position without the monetary risk of being self-employed. Of course, they forfeit the freedom of being their own bosses.

Many consultants are corporate drop-outs. Kim T. Gordon quit her job as marketing vice-president of a large real estate sales company to start her home-based business, Marketing and Communications Counsel. Gordon offers strategic planning services in marketing and communications. In her first year of business, she earned $15,000 more in personal income than she had earned working for someone else. Gordon has total control over her time and her business. Though the business is growing, she wants to continue to run it from her home—a feat made possible by computer technology and other electronic tools.

Sources of additional information for consultants

Numerous publications are available to those interested in consulting as a profession. Consultants are listed in a number of directories, including *Dun's Consultant's Directory* and *Consultants and Consulting Organizations Directory,* found in the reference section of many libraries. *Consultants News* and the *Journal of Management Consulting* are periodicals covering up-to-date information in the field. Some associations for consultants include:

American Consultants League
640 S. Washington Boulevard
Sarasota, FL 34236

American Association of
   Professional Consultants
9140 Ward Parkway
Kansas City, MO 64114

Association of Management
   Consulting Firms (ACME)
230 Park Avenue
New York, NY 10169

(ACME provides the *Directory of ACME Member Firms Interested in Receiving Resumes from Candidates* to job seekers.)

Association of Management
   Consultants
500 N. Michigan Avenue
Chicago, IL 60611

Council of Consulting
   Organizations
230 Park Avenue
New York, NY 10169

The Institute of Management
  Consultants (IMC)
19 West 44th Street, #810
New York, NY 10036

National Association of
  Professional Consultants
20121 Ventura Boulevard
Woodland Hills, CA 91364

(Members of IMC include ACME firms, public accounting firms, small firms, and independent consultants. The organization offers a three-day course, Fundamentals of Management Consulting, and certifies its members as Certified Management Consultants [CMC].)

Professional and Technical
  Consultants Association
1330 S. Bascom Avenue, Suite D
San Jose, CA 95128

Society of Professional
  Management Consultants
136 Engle Street
Englewood, NJ 07631

ENTREPRENEURSHIP

The Job

It has been said that the only way most people are ever going to make a million dollars is by starting their own businesses. Entrepreneurs are individuals who are willing to assume personal and financial risks to do just that. The demand for a product or service creates an opportunity for prospective entrepreneurs. In addition to making money, the entrepreneur has the freedom to run the company in his or her own way. However, small businesses are built on more than dreams of money and independence. A tremendous amount of knowledge and effort is involved. Starting a business is difficult; staying in business is harder still.

Entrepreneurs must identify a marketable product. The only limit is one's imagination. Parents can play a role in encouraging their children to be creative and entrepreneurial. For example, Gilman Louie's parents denied him and his brothers store-bought toys. Rather, they provided the materials for the boys to make their own toys. As a teen, Louie began creating computer games, started his own company in his sophomore year of college, and sold 80 percent of it for roughly $1 million seven years later.

Ideas come from many sources. For example, 1,400-pound Walter Hudson got stuck in a doorway in 1987 and had to be sawed free. Though he has lost half that weight since then, he was well aware of the problems finding clothes for persons weighing from 200 to 1,000 pounds. He began Walter Hudson Ventures, Inc., a mail-order firm that sells designer clothes to women in that weight range. In his first nine months of business, sales reached $1 million, with a good profit for Hudson. Then there's the success story of Hawk and Animal, two wrestlers whose company grossed $20 million last year selling wild, baggy trousers dubbed Zubaz pants—Zubaz being a sports put-down meaning "in your face."

If a market exists, smart business people can sell just about anything. Even revenge is for sale these days. Such consultants as Lesa Patrock of

Local Revenge and Alan Abel, who offers a course entitled "Don't Get Mad, Get Even," suggest creative methods of retaliation against coworkers who are chronically late, chain-smoke in the office, steal office supplies, or engage in other annoying or dishonest activities.

Using the same technique employed by large companies, independent entrepreneurs find a market niche, develop a product, and market it. For example, Richard Worth capitalized on the recent emphasis on nutrition by selling first "healthy" jam, then "healthy" cookies. His company, R.W. Frookies, Inc., sells whole-grain cookies sweetened with fruit juice. While employed as a marketing consultant, Worth and his wife, a nutritionist, put their heads together and developed recipes and a business plan. He raised money from suppliers and distributors to begin the company. In two years his company rocketed to $18 million in sales. This was not accomplished through luck alone. A tremendous amount of knowledge and effort is required to develop a successful small business such as this. Worth still works from 12 to 16 hours a day—the norm for successful small-business owners. Speaking of cookies, Debbi Fields opened her first store in 1977 at age 20 with a $50,000 loan from a banker who liked her chocolate chip cookies. Ten years later, Mrs. Fields Inc. was a company of 543 stores in six countries including Japan and Australia.

Aptitudes and Attributes Needed for Success

Because of the large investment of time and money and the high risk of failure, an entrepreneur must have a total commitment to the business, a tolerance for hard work, good health, and financial backing in order to succeed. The prospective entrepreneur usually seeks financial backing from relatives, friends, and lending institutions. Normally entrepreneurs put a good bit of their own money into their businesses. If they have developed an impressive business plan, they may be successful in getting financial backing from outside sources such as banks or venture capitalists.

Venture capital firms are usually groups of investors who extend financial backing to start-up companies in exchange for partial ownership of the company, which varies from arrangement to arrangement. Usually the venture capital firm wants to protect its investment by having considerable say in how the company is run. Given that the idea is good, raising capital for high-tech businesses is somewhat easier than for other small businesses. This is not to say that many high-tech businesses do not go under, but the growth and potential profits in high-tech areas are appealing enough to venture capitalists to offset the risk. Many fledgling businesses fail because they are underfinanced and lack sufficient capital to remain in business long enough to turn a profit. Even so, many small-business owners have taken on the risk of starting their own businesses in order to have total freedom to run them as they see fit. When this is the case, the entrepreneur attempts to go it alone, without venture capital.

Though securing financial backing is often the stumbling block beyond which hopeful entrepreneurs cannot pass, more than money is required to make a business go. Once finances are secured, an entrepreneur begins to implement the business plan. Since in most small businesses, the owner is responsible for planning, accounting, purchasing, producing, marketing, staffing, and overall management, a general knowledge of all the activities of business is required. Above all, an entrepreneur must be a salesperson extraordinaire—first selling the idea in order to raise the capital to start the company, then selling the company and its future to prospective employees, and finally selling the product to consumers who are constantly bombarded with ideas for new and better products. Such attributes as a willingness to face risk, to work long hours, to tolerate the uncertainty of success during the early stages of the business, and to keep thorough records in order to fill out the numerous forms required by the government—all these are needed to be a successful entrepreneur. Communications skills, a dominant presence, and a high energy level are necessary personal traits for a successful entrepreneur. The entrepreneur is of a rare breed, both resilient and tough—flexible enough to change plans when advantageous and strong enough to handle the disappointments and problems that plague all who go into business for themselves.

Current Trends

Small businesses contribute greatly to the health of the U.S. economy, creating both products and jobs. The 1980s experienced an entrepreneurial boom, with a dramatic increase in new business start-ups and a doubling of the number of incorporations between 1975 and 1986. Recent declines in the growth rate of new businesses are attributed largely to growing unease about the economy. Certain types of businesses anticipate hard times. For example, independent restauranteurs have been consistently losing ground to the top 100 chains since 1972. The total number of restaurants is declining due to competition and a saturated market. Small manufacturers whose processes involve chemical emissions and waste are concerned that they will have difficulty complying with a host of new government environmental regulations affecting small businesses.

Other types of businesses are more optimistic. Romance is in, and many small-business owners are loving it. Photographers, musicians, florists, tailors, and caterers are cashing in on the $30-billion-a-year wedding business. Although the pool of young people in their prime marriage years is decreasing, marriages among older individuals and repeat marriages will help sustain the market, and interest in big, elegant bashes has remained strong. Small independent bookstores have grown in numbers over the past five years as readers' preferences grow more specialized. The point is that entrepreneurs should be aware of market and economic conditions if they hope to succeed, and these conditions are changing constantly.

Sources of Additional Information for Entrepreneurs

Usually small family businesses employ family members in key positions. If the business has a board of directors, it is composed of family members. Thus, the question of where to get objective advice on small-business matters arises. The Small Business Administration (SBA), which has offices in all major cities, is an excellent source of information for those who want to start their own businesses or need help once they have set up shop. Numerous brochures published by SBA are available in SBA offices around the country or may be requested by mail. These brochures give valuable how-to information, such as developing a business plan, acquiring financing, marketing products, and much more. Many books on managing small businesses are in print.

Small-business consultants offer services to small-business owners who can afford them. A source of advice for businesses with annual revenues of at least $2 million and at least 25 employees is a San Diego-based company called Executive Committee Inc., which organizes sessions for groups of executives from small companies. These sessions consist of a presentation by a business expert and a problem-solving session during which the executives help one another find solutions to problems. Membership in an executive group is by invitation and costs $7,600 per year.

Information and assistance for small business owners can be obtained by writing to the following:

Chamber of Commerce of the
   United States
1615 H Street N.W.
Washington, D.C. 20006

National Association of Small
   Business Investment Companies
1156 Fifteenth Street N.W.
Washington, D.C. 20005

National Association of Women
   Business Owners
500 N. Michigan Avenue, Suite
   1400
Chicago, IL 60611

National Federation of
   Independent Business
150 W. 20th Avenue
San Mateo, CA 94403

SWAP Club International
P.O. Box 149
Arvada, CO 80001

U.S. Small Business
   Administration
1441 L. Street N.W.
Washington, D.C. 20016

The Small Business Administration offers a wide range of publications useful to those interested in starting small businesses or running them profitably. SBA offices are located in cities around the country, and toll-free telephone numbers are available for people who live in towns without an SBA office.

CAREERS IN FRANCHISING

The Job

Many people want to own their own small businesses but lack an original idea for a product choose to buy a franchise. A franchise can be defined as an agreement between a small-business owner, called a *franchisee,* and a parent company, termed a *franchisor,* that gives the owner the right to sell the company's product (goods or services) under conditions agreed upon by both. The store itself is also called a franchise. A great many small retail stores are franchises, including fast food restaurants, gas stations, print shops, and other stores selling almost every type of good or service. Statistics show that the proportionate number of failures among franchises is significantly less than among other independent businesses. Certain advantages to franchises help minimize the risk of failure.

Advantages.   Failure in a franchise is reduced by the nature of the franchise itself. First of all, franchises sell nationally known and extensively tested products for which a market has already been established. Second, training and assistance from the parent company help the new owner choose a location, set up shop, estimate potential sales, and design market strategies that have worked in similar locations. Finally, cooperative buying power enables the franchise owner to get supplies at lower costs from distributors that supply all franchises of the parent company. Sometimes the parent company helps to get credit for the new franchise, since it generally takes a new business at least six months to turn a profit. However, these advantages do not guarantee success. Even franchises of a successful parent company sometimes fail. Regardless of the services and training that a franchisor offers a franchisee, a good rule of thumb is that any prospective small business owner should have all the business knowledge and skills to go into business entirely on his or her own.

Disadvantages.   There are disadvantages to owning a franchise. Franchise owners pay a franchising fee plus a percentage of their profits to the parent company. This percentage is determined by the amount of advertising and consulting support given by the parent company and varies considerably. It can range from 3 percent to a whopping 50 percent in the temporary-help business. However, in the temporary-help business, the franchisor finances the payrolls of the franchisees. Though the requirement that the owner buy both equipment and supplies from vendors specified by the parent company is often advantageous, this is not always the case. Arrangements vary. A unique disadvantage to the franchise arrangement is that sometimes parent companies fail, bringing down all franchise stores as well, no matter how well an individual store might be faring.

In the relationship between franchisor and franchisee, the bargaining position of the franchisee is far less than that of the franchisor. Thus, caution should be exercised before entering into an agreement. A prospective owner first should read the fine print and get legal advice as well. The law requires that franchisors must provide a detailed franchise prospectus to potential franchisees. It is wise to keep in mind that the business of the parent company is selling franchises. Like all businesses, it is going to make the product—in this case, the franchise—as appealing as possible. The potential profits as well as estimated costs of setting up the franchise stated by the parent company should be assessed by questioning other franchise owners as well as objective sources. The Federal Trade Commission requires that franchisors divulge any litigation in which they are involved. Because fraudulent claims and franchise scams are on the rise, a franchise agreement should be entered into carefully with legal advice and as much outside knowledge of the parent company as possible.

Current Trends

More than one-third of retail dollars are spent in franchised businesses today, and predictions are that more than half of all retail sales in the 1990s will be generated by franchises. Although such old-line franchises as hotels, fast food restaurants, and car rental agencies have reached a saturation point, new opportunities in business and professional services are available. Manufacturers are franchising aspects of the distribution process, such as sales territories and delivery routes, to reduce overhead. More franchise opportunities will be available today, partially because it costs less for a company to franchise today than it did 15 years ago. Uniform disclosure documents are accepted in all states reducing legal fees. The cost to franchise can range from $100,000 to $200,000.

From the standpoint of the franchisee, most franchises cost from $50,000 to $250,000 to start, with the average being $140,000. Home-based franchises can run as low as $10,000. The most expensive franchises can cost as much as $10 million. The percentage of these costs required in cash varies with current credit conditions and ranges from 20 percent to 40 percent when money is tight. The remaining percentage can be bank-financed and pledged with personal guarantees and collateral. Franchise agreements are not to be entered into lightly. The monetary cost of failure can be considerable.

The current failure rate for franchises is estimated at about 10 percent per year. This figure includes both franchises that go out of business and those that have been bought out by the franchisor or another franchisee. Franchises fail for many reasons. Lack of financing to support the business until it becomes profitable may cause failure. Even with services and training provided by the franchisor, some owners simply lack the skills required to run a successful business. Often investors buy franchises and hire others to run them, but incentives are different for paid employees than for owners and thus, lack of involvement by the investor is often cited as the reason for business failure. Sometimes the parent company goes under, causing all franchisees to shut down—successful or not.

Sources of Additional Information on Franchising

There are numerous sources of information on franchises. The *Franchise Opportunities Handbook,* published by the Bureau of Industrial Economics and Minority Business Development Agency of the U.S. Department of Commerce, can be found in the government documents section of most libraries. Published monthly, it includes a list of franchises for sale as well as excellent tips for prospective franchise owners, such as a checklist for evaluating a franchise, financial assistance information, and a bibliography of sources of franchising information. Other sources include the following:

Directory of Franchise Business Opportunities
Franchise Business Opportunities Publishing Company
1725 Washington Road, Suite 205
Pittsburgh, PA 15241

Directory of Franchising Organizations
Pilot Industries, Inc.
347 Fifth Avenue
New York, NY 10016

The Franchise Annual
Info Press
736 Center Street
Lewiston, NY 14092

International Franchise Association
1025 Connecticut Avenue N.W. Suite 1005
Washington, D.C. 20036

The directories listed herein are revised annually and provide information on many franchise opportunities. These franchises should be thoroughly checked out by contacting both the Better Business Bureau and the International Franchise Association. Many excellent books on franchising are on the market, a number of them available through the International Franchise Association itself.

INTEREST ANALYSIS CHART

Consider what you have just learned about education, consulting, and business ownership—both as an entrepreneur and as a franchisee. In an effort to analyze your interest in these areas as options for further along your career path, complete Figure 10-3, the interest analysis chart. In identifying the pros and cons of education, consulting, and business ownership, think in personal terms. Focus on what appeals or does not appeal to you in terms of your identified aptitudes, interests, and values.

Figure 10-3— Interest analysis chart

Education

Personal pros	Personal cons
1.	1.
2.	2.
3.	3.
4.	4.

Consulting

Personal pros	Personal cons
1.	1.
2.	2.
3.	3.
4.	4.

Business ownership

Personal pros	Personal cons
1.	1.
2.	2.
3.	3.
4.	4.

WHAT NEXT?

Throughout the first 10 chapters, you have learned a great deal about careers in business. Chapter 11 is designed to help you select a field using the career evaluations at the ends of the chapters. Also included are suggestions on how to research industries and companies to determine where your best opportunities probably will lie.

SELECTING YOUR BUSINESS CAREER

CHAPTER OBJECTIVES

Upon completion of this chapter, you should be able to:

1. Select a career in business using the career decision-making model.
2. Discuss some of the pros and cons of work in government, not-for-profit, and profit-seeking organizations.
3. Research industries to determine where the best future opportunities will lie.
4. Locate information on specific companies in selecting from employment alternatives.

The culmination of your decision-making process occurs in this chapter. You are now ready to put together the pieces of your career puzzle. After that, the rest will fall into place for you. Your career decision-making model and the career evaluations that you completed throughout this book will enable you to select a career in business that will satisfy your personal career requirements.

PUTTING TOGETHER THE CAREER PUZZLE

The time has come to select your career in business. You have systematically investigated a number of career areas throughout this book and focused on some specific jobs in those areas. Use the Job Rank form in this chapter to reconsider those jobs according to the following instructions:

1. Look back at Figure 2-2, Career Evaluation Model for Accounting, near the end of Chapter 2. Examine the completed Career Evaluation form. You entered a specific job at the top of the form. Write this job in the column entitled *Job* on the Job Rank form in the space to the right of the word "accounting." Follow this procedure for entering jobs from each Career Evaluation form for the remaining chapters through Chapter 9.
2. Examine the jobs you have listed. In the column entitled *Subjective rank,* rank the jobs in the order of your preference from 1 to 8, with 1 entered beside the job you most prefer and 8 the job you least prefer. *Use only your gut feeling to do this!*
3. Now look at the Career Summary form in this chapter. Enter the jobs from the *Job* column on the Job Rank form into the *Job* column on the Career Summary form.
4. Turn to the completed Career Evaluation form in Chapter 2 again. Enter the totals from each of the six groups of factors into

JOB RANK				
Chapter	Career area	Job	Subjective rank	Objective rank
2	Accounting			
3	Computers and information technology			
4	Finance			
5	Insurance and real estate			
6	Marketing			
7	Operations, production, and materials management			
8	Human resource management			
9	Management and supervision			

the appropriate columns ("Aptitudes and attributes," "Interests," and so on) on the Career Summary form. Repeat this step for each chapter through Chapter 9.

5. Sum up the points for each job by adding points for all factors across the row horizontally. Enter the sum in the column entitled *Overall total* on the Career Summary form. Do this for each of the eight jobs.

6. Return to the Job Rank form and the column entitled *Objective rank*. Rank the jobs from 1 to 8 according to the overall total points that you entered for each job on the Career Summary form. Let 1 indicate the job with the most points and 8 the job with the least points.

7. Carefully compare the subjective rank and the objective rank for each job.

If this book were a novel, the activity you have just completed would be considered the climax. Now let's see if you have resolved the career dilemma. Does each job that you have listed carry the same subjective and objective rank, or do the ranks differ? What about the number 1 job preferred at the gut level? Is this job also number 1 in the objective analysis resulting from the use of the career decision-making model? If both your gut feeling and the objective analysis produced the same number 1 job, you have very likely ended up with a solid basis for planning your career

CAREER SUMMARY

Chapter	Career area	Job	Internal factors			External factors			Overall total
			Aptitudes and attributes	Interests	Values	Family influence	Economic influence	Societal influence	
2	Accounting								
3	Computers and information technology								
4	Finance								
5	Insurance and real estate								
6	Marketing								
7	Production and materials management								
8	Human resources management and public relations								
9	Management and supervision								

path and an excellent career choice. But don't be disappointed if a discrepancy occurred. Probably more often than not, the ranks will differ, even on the number 1 job. This does not mean that you have wasted your time. It simply means that you have to do a little more analysis before selecting your career area.

Consider how many people choose careers. They act on a few pieces of information and gut feeling or intuition. Few engage in the systematic analysis that you have done throughout the course of this book. Even your subjective rank for each job was based on an evaluation of a considerable amount of information. The job ranked number 1 according to your gut feeling may be the one for you even though it differs from the number 1 job in the objective analysis. At this point, you must be sure because your career decision may well be the most important decision of your life so far.

One reason why many individuals change college majors or make drastic career changes that require them to return to college for complete retooling is that their career choices have been too subjective, often unrealistic for them personally. Look at your number 1 job from subjective rank and your number 1 job from objective rank. If they are the same, there's no problem. If they differ, use the Career Summary form to compare the two number 1 jobs. It is possible that you are weighing certain factors in your mind as being more important than the weights that you assigned to them in your model and some factors as less important. The numbers should reveal this to you. You may have to return to the Career Evaluation forms at the ends of the chapters for each of the jobs and compare them.

It is up to you to reconcile your job choice now. You may want to reread some chapters. You may want to look more closely at the job that ranked number 2 in your objective analysis. You may want to consider some of the individual factors in the model and weigh them again in your mind. If you haven't already written for additional information from some of the sources listed in each chapter, you may want to do that before making a career choice.

Before planning your educational program, you should feel fairly comfortable with your career choice. You should then begin to look at various types of organizations and specific industries so that you can tailor your career preparation for entry into an organization or industry that both interests you and is likely to provide opportunities for you in the future.

GOVERNMENT, NOT-FOR-PROFIT, AND PROFIT-SEEKING ORGANIZATIONS

There are numerous trade-offs in opting for jobs in government, not-for-profit, and profit-seeking organizations. If security is a top priority or you want to move along with practically guaranteed promotions, you might want to consider government jobs. In general, government positions at local, state, and federal levels are increasing in numbers as new agencies are being created to deal with complex environmental, technological, and social problems. Although salaries are somewhat lower than in private industry in most cases, a step procedure based on tenure and a series of examinations assures that salary increases and movement to the next higher step will come at fairly predictable times. Of course, this is a lockstep procedure and advancing a few levels in a single leap is not usual for government employees. Still, increasing opportunities, practically guaranteed advancement, and very rare layoffs make government jobs very attractive to those who value security highly.

Positions in not-for-profit organizations such as charities, churches, and trade or professional associations do not offer the security of government jobs. Still, many well-established not-for-profit organizations are highly stable with fairly constant or increasing membership and financial support even in economic slumps. Such organizations offer greater security than many private industries. Although profit sharing is not a possibility since there are essentially no profits made and income is restricted to salary, there is evidence that salaries are becoming somewhat competitive with private industry. In the past, almost all graduates of top business schools in the country went into private industry. Recently, there has been some change. A number of these graduates are accepting positions with not-for-profit organizations today. Apart from the altruism and sense of professionalism associated with working for not-for-profit organizations, individuals are building solid careers and gaining many associations with influential individuals in the private sector should they choose to make a career move into private industry.

Working for profit-seeking organizations offers opportunities for rapid advancement and often an ability to benefit economically in line with the company profits. Profit sharing, bonuses, commissions, and other fringe benefits make private industry financially attractive. However, the futures of these profit-seeking organizations are inextricably linked to such factors as general economic conditions, environment, technology, consumer preference, and a host of other things. Positions are usually not guaranteed or protected by tenure at professional levels, advancement within the company may or may not occur, and companies do fold. Stability and growth potential—both in entire industries and within specific companies—are important considerations for individuals who choose to build their careers in private industry.

RESEARCHING INDUSTRIES AND COMPANIES

One of the most valuable sources of occupational information is the *Occupational Outlook Handbook* produced by the U.S. Bureau of Labor Statistics. Included in it are approximately 300 occupational briefs which are grouped into 13 clusters of related jobs. These briefs include the same kinds of information covered in this book. The *Occupational Outlook Handbook* also provides information on industries. Industries are analyzed for job opportunities in 35 industry briefs. According to the Bureau of Labor Statistics, 9 of every 10 new jobs created in the next 10 years will be in the service industries, with the health and computer industries growing the fastest. Business services, in general, have averaged a 20 percent growth rate.

Very often the January issues of business publications such as *Business Week* and *Forbes* provide an industrial outlook for the coming year. The forecasts focus on growth and sales. Since it is hard for people entering jobs in private industry to avoid specializing by industry to some extent, it is wise for job seekers to identify a healthy industry in which to build a career.

There are numerous reliable sources of industry information. *Standard & Poor's Industry Surveys* cover 69 major domestic industries. Usually found in the reference section of the library, the *Surveys* include current and basic analyses. The current analysis includes latest industry developments; industry, market, and company statistics; and appraisals of investment outlook. The basic analysis includes prospects for the particular industry, an analysis of trends and problems, spotlights on major segments of the industry, growth in sales and earnings of leading companies in the industry, and other information over a 10-year span.

Another excellent source of industry information is *The Value Line Investment Survey* published weekly by Arnold Bernhard and Co., Inc., in New York. The most up-to-date information on industries and companies is covered in this survey.

Many sources focus on specific companies. *The Dun & Bradstreet Directories, Moody's Manuals,* and *Thomas's Register* all provide specific company information such as the address and phone number of the company, what the business produces, annual sales, and names of officers and directors. *Dun & Bradstreet* covers a wide variety of concerns with net worth of from $500,000 to over $1 million. *Thomas's Register* lists manufacturing companies. *Moody's* lists firms whose securities are traded.

It is possible to focus on a company's officers and directors to learn names, addresses, dates of birth, education, current positions, and sometimes former business positions held. Two sources for this type of information are *Standard & Poor's Register of Corporations, Directors, and Executives* and *Dun & Bradstreet's Reference Book of Corporate Managements*. These books are especially useful for an understanding of who makes it to the top in a particular company and what kind of education and experience were required to do it.

For people who are ready to apply for jobs, the sources described above can be used to research companies that list job openings. One source of published job openings readily available in college libraries and career information centers is the *College Placement Annual*. This annual

lists the occupational needs anticipated by approximately 1,000 corporations and employers who normally recruit college graduates. One section
of the *Annual* lists companies alphabetically and includes phone, contact
person, products and services, year the company was established, the
number of employees, what positions are available, and the location of
the available positions. Another section of the *Annual* lists the U.S. government agency openings. Also included in the *Annual* are sections in
which companies are grouped according to occupational area—for example, accounting—and geographically, by state. The *College Placement
Annual* even provides excellent information on job seeking in general,
such as interviewing and resume-writing hints.

For MBAs, an excellent publication entitled *Careers and the MBA* is
produced by the Harvard Business School. Featured in it are articles discussing specific careers; industry reports that give an overview of the industry, opportunities, and trends; and excellent bibliographies for use in
researching careers. Articles and industry reports are written by representatives of firms participating in the production of *Careers and the
MBA*. Also listed is a description of these firms, their career opportunities, and current recruiting contact addresses. If this publication is not
available in your library or college information center, it can be ordered
by writing:

Careers and the MBA
Morris V
Harvard Business School
Boston, MA 02163

ONE LAST STEP

Now that you have made a career decision, even a tentative decision, and
know some available sources for researching industries, companies, and
job opportunities, you are ready to prepare yourself for a competitive
market. Chapter 12 will suggest some tips for planning your college program, gaining communication skills, preparing a resume, and interviewing for jobs.

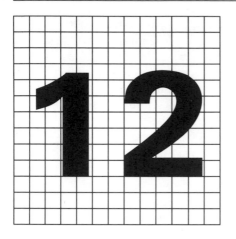

PREPARING YOURSELF FOR A COMPETITIVE MARKET

CHAPTER OBJECTIVES

Upon completion of this chapter, you should be able to:

1. Plan a college program that will prepare you for the career that you selected.

2. Describe the importance of communication skills for success in business and how to acquire them.

3. Prepare a resume that will appeal to prospective employers.

4. Conduct yourself in an interview situation so that you make a positive impression on the interviewer and gain the information you need to evaluate your career possibilities with the company.

5. Consider the kinds of decisions that may influence your future career.

If you are comfortable with your career decision at this point, you have come a long way indeed. The hardest part—making the decision—is over. The rest is rather routine by comparison. This chapter is designed to give you some career planning hints on how to stay on top of the competition.

TAILORING YOUR EDUCATION FOR SUCCESS

Having focused on a career area and even a specific job that interests you, you must now plan your educational program to give you the best possible preparation for entering your chosen field. Your college major should be fairly obvious, but that is only part of your educational plan. You have, in addition to your major, choices of a minor and elective courses. These choices are very important. Now that you have chosen a career goal, *make every college course that you take a step toward achieving that goal.*

Begin by rereading the entire chapter that discusses careers in your chosen area. Focus particularly on the sections entitled *The Job* and *Aptitudes and Attributes Needed for Success.* Attempt to identify specific areas of competency needed for success in your job. Often courses were suggested. Carefully look at the attributes needed for success in your career. List courses that might help you develop these areas of competency and attributes. Add them to your program. Even if you must remain in college an extra quarter or semester to complete these courses, it may be worth it, especially if your field is fairly competitive.

Know the importance of every course in your college program to your career goals. A favorite area that job interviewers address is the college program—courses taken, the value of them, the ones enjoyed most. Go into your interviews able to articulate this in relation to your career goals. Your planning and preparation will impress any interviewer and set you apart from the other applicants.

Your education certainly will not be restricted to college courses. Any involvement in student organizations, cooperative work experience or internship programs, and indeed, work experience of all kinds will prove very valuable to you in business.

If you fail to see the relevance of membership in student organizations, even primarily social ones, to your career preparation, look again. One quality that all interviewers are looking for is leadership potential. Holding office in a student organization is very impressive for an individual who plans to enter the world of business. The ability to get along with others and to influence them is crucial to your success. Being active in student organizations will give you an opportunity to develop these abilities and put them to the test. Remember, people who opt for business careers do not work alone in a controlled laboratory setting, but rather in the real world dealing with every imaginable type of person. Every group affiliation will help you develop the polish you need, so don't pass up any opportunities.

College-sponsored cooperative work experience or internship programs provide tremendous career opportunities for college students. The experience of applying the knowledge you have gained in courses to real problems and situations is invaluable. Along with the experience, you will work under a supervisor who may write an important letter of recommendation for you—one based not only on your academic ability, but also on your competence to perform a job.

Holding down *any job* for a period of time impresses a prospective employer. This work experience demonstrates responsibility, stability, maturity, an ability to work with others, and an acceptance of authority. These qualities are premiums and are hard to determine from college grade point averages.

No one will ever tell you that your grade point average is not important. It is a somewhat objective measure that enables a prospective employer to compare you with other applicants. It is, however, not the only criterion for selection and is used in conjunction with many other factors. In business, employers want well-rounded employees who perform well in a variety of situations. Because it is the total person who is hired, not the academician or the socialite, you must work to balance your educational experiences among numerous alternatives to develop the widest range of competence. Be sure to note any specific suggestions made in the chapter discussing your chosen career area.

GAINING COMMUNICATION SKILLS

You doubtless have noticed that communication skills are stressed as a necessary requirement for success in all careers in business. Expressing yourself clearly in writing and speaking becomes increasingly more important as you move upward through the management levels of the company. Writing reports and proposals, as well as presenting them to groups both inside and outside the organization, is a requirement of most business professionals. Speeches by company executives to influential groups outside the organization can have a substantial impact on the organization's future.

Colleges offer many writing and public speaking courses. A course in written business communications is sometimes offered by the college of business. If you know that you lack communication skills, you would be wise to enroll in these courses to correct your deficiencies before they work against you in finding a job or being promoted. Any opportunities to gain experience in delivering speeches or conducting meetings offered through membership in student organizations is greatly encouraged.

You will begin to realize the value of your communication skills even before you begin to work. During resume preparation and interviewing, you will draw upon these skills to sell yourself to prospective employers and gain for yourself the greatest number of career options. Remember, what people use to evaluate you is what you communicate to them!

FINDING THE RIGHT JOB

Books have been written on the subject of finding the right job. One of the best and most widely used is *What Color Is Your Parachute?* by Richard Nelson Bolles, published by Ten Speed Press of Berkeley, California. You can find it in almost every bookstore including college campus bookstores. Buy it! It will help to insulate you against some of the disappointments and frustrations of the job search and help you organize your search so that you don't waste time and energy on things that rarely, if ever, pay off. Another helpful book is *How to Land a Better Job,* by Catherine and Oscar Lott, published by NTC Publishing Group of Lincolnwood, Illinois. This book will provide you with practical advice and ways of dealing with job choices.

The college placement office organizes on-campus interviews for students with many major companies. You should take advantage of every opportunity to meet company representatives while they are on campus. They are recruiting you; therefore, the psychological advantage is yours. Many college placement offices require completion of student data sheets or college interview forms, which are forwarded to the interviewers so that they may better prepare for the interview. The information is roughly the same as is found on the resume. Resumes also may be used. The following sections provide hints for resume preparation and job interviewing.

A RESUME THAT WORKS FOR YOU

If you have selected a job, identified an industry, and determined the type of company for which you would like to work, only then are you ready to write a resume. Your resume is a summary of your education, work experience, interests, career goals, and any other information that qualifies you for the particular position that you seek.

Format

How you organize the information on your resume depends on how you feel you can best promote yourself. *There is no best way!*

One alternative format is a chronological arrangement of educational and work experiences, each listed separately with the most recent experience first. A second alternative is a resume organized around competencies to do the job. Define the competency, such as "Conducting Research" or "Writing Computer Programs in FORTRAN", and under each stated competency write courses or experiences through which you gained the competency. This second alternative is especially valuable for beginners who have very little work experience. It is also effective for job seekers who have periods of time during which they were neither working outside the home nor in school, such as full-time mothers returning to work as their children grow older.

The resume may use phrases or complete sentences. In either case, it should be neat, attractive, and well-spaced, with headings that stand out.

Content

Although the specific content of the resume depends on the individual, certain categories of information have become fairly standard for inclusion in resumes. These categories will be discussed briefly in the following paragraphs.

Personal information. Your full name, address, and phone number are requirements. Such information as height, weight, age, race, place of birth, marital status, dependents, military status, sexual orientation, health, and physical handicaps should not be included on the resume. It is illegal for an employer to ask for personal information that is unrelated to the job, and volunteering certain information actually might prejudice an employer against you.

Career objective. Stated concisely, your career objective can strengthen your resume. It should be broad enough to include a number of related jobs and to interest a number of employers, but it should point out a definite career direction.

Education. The highest level of education should be listed first. Each degree and relevant educational experience should show dates, degree or certificate earned, and major or area in which it was earned. Any honors such as awards, dean's list, *better than average* grades, or offices held in college also should be included. If you have over three honors to list, use a separate category entitled *Honors and Activities* or whatever title seems appropriate to what you intend to include.

Work experience   All work experience should be included in your resume when you are beginning your career. Internships, volunteer work, and summer jobs may be used. Emphasize the degree of responsibility held and the skills demonstrated. You may organize your work experience chronologically, listing your most recent work experience first and working backward, or you may organize it around competencies as suggested earlier. This would give you the opportunity to list courses as well as experience to demonstrate certain skills. For the individual with very little work experience or a very specific career direction, this is a good way to sell yourself. An explanation of your work experience should include your employer, your position, dates of employment, and duties performed.

References.   *Do not list the names and addresses of your references on your resume.* Instead, write "Available upon request" or "Available from college placement office upon request" if you are registered with the placement office. It is a wise idea to set up a placement file if you are a beginner or think that you will apply to many companies. Rather than asking your references to send letters to each company, you may have them send a letter to your college placement office. The letter will be placed in a file and be duplicated and sent to employers upon your request.

Hints

Keep in mind the following hints in writing your resume.

1. People usually skim resumes. Too many numbers, too much verbiage, poor spacing, and unclear headings all make a resume difficult to skim.

2. No matter how terrific you are or how much experience you have had, your resume should not be longer than three pages. If you can say it in one or two, so much the better. The resume will be used to determine whether to interview you. If you write a resume that kindles an employer's interest, you can really light some fires in the interview that will follow.

3. Employers are looking at tone and content. Be positive; absolutely nothing negative should appear in your resume. Use action verbs such as "coordinated," "supervised," and "developed." Emphasize skills and highlight experiences relevant to the position you seek.

4. Use an individually typed cover letter each time you send a resume to a prospective employer. Introduce yourself, explain your reason for writing, describe what contributions you feel you can make to the organization, and request an interview.

5. Seek out help from the pros in your campus career information center who will assist you in writing your resume and make information on resume writing and sample resumes available to you.

6. Keep copies of all letters you send out in one file folder, all responses requiring action on your part in a second folder, and all rejection letters in a third folder.

7. An interested employer often responds with a phone call rather than a letter. Keep a pad and pen beside the phone so that you can thoroughly record all essential information. The more organized and in control you appear to be, the more you will impress prospective employers.

THE INTERVIEW

If you have made it this far—defined a career objective, prepared yourself, organized your job search, and written an excellent resume—don't relax and lose the race on the last lap! No matter how smooth and polished you are, you have to prepare yourself carefully for every interview.

Get ready

Getting ready for the job interview does not mean simply getting dressed up. It means gaining a thorough knowledge of your potential employer and what you have to offer as a prospective employee. You should know such things as the products or services that the organization provides, the size and growth potential of the organization, the organization's executives and their backgrounds, and the current market position of the company within its industry. Use the sources described in Chapter 11 to research a company and its executives.

Gain as much knowledge as you can about the specific position opening before the interview. You might ask the coordinator of the college placement service for information. Often companies organize booklets or folders of information about the organization and its employees which are housed in the placement office. This information might increase your knowledge of the requirements of the position.

Once you have a reasonable idea of the skills required and the overall responsibilities of the job, analyze your own educational background and work experience in terms of these skills and responsibilities to be ready to discuss this with an interviewer. It is important that you be able to see the position as a step along the career path you have outlined for yourself. You should be able to talk about your short- and long-term career objectives, your interests, and your strengths and weaknesses.

Get set

Set yourself up for a successful interview by making sure that your first impression on the interviewer is a good one because it *will* be a lasting one. Neat, conservative dress is recommended. Women should wear a simply tailored suit, a neat hairstyle, plain jewelry, and moderate makeup and perfume. Men should wear a conservative suit, shirt, and tie. Polished shoes, trimmed and styled hair, and clean fingernails contribute to a man's overall appearance.

Be early rather than late. If you are late, the interviewer will have less time to spend with you and you will be unable to make as many points in your favor. Also, if you arrive late, your reliability might be questioned.

Attempt to project a courteous and enthusiastic image. You should be looking forward to the interview as an opportunity to promote yourself and to gain information about the company and the position available. If you have prepared yourself and are confident in your appearance, you will be calm, not nervous, and able to look upon the interview as the opportunity that it is.

Go

Although each interview will be unique, there are usually four phases in an interview. The first phase is devoted to breaking the ice and establishing a climate for the exchange of information. It may involve humor, small talk, and a few simple questions that clarify items on your resume.

The second phase of the interview is the hard part. During this phase, the interviewer will attempt to get as much information from you as possible. Always remember that the interviewer controls the interview. Be patient and answer all questions carefully. You will have an opportunity to ask your questions before the interview is complete. Your responses to the interviewer's questions demonstrate your performance under pressure, quickness, effectiveness, energy, sense of humor, and grammar. Expect some broad questions, such as "How would you describe yourself as a person?" and "How can you contribute to our organization?" Remember that the interviewer is looking at both substance, which is basically your past performance, and style, which includes communications skills, poise, self-confidence, and motivation. Broad questions reveal how you organize your thoughts; your values; your personality; and even what you might be like to work with.

No matter how mentally exhausted you are after answering the interviewer's questions, summon some energy for the third phase of the interview, because it's your turn to ask the questions. The interviewer probably will ask if you have any questions. You always should! Such topics as training possibilities, and other opportunities for professional growth, advancement possibilities, the average age of persons in the next level up in the company, and how many people were hired in the last few recruiting seasons are all things you might like to know. Focus on *opportunities* for your professional growth and work-related activities. Wait until the job is offered to you before you ask questions about such things as vacations or retirement.

The final phase may be a summary of what has been said, an indication of when you should expect to hear from the company, and friendly words of departure. You should remember to thank the interviewer. The interest in you shown by the interviewer does not mean that you will get the job. It is standard operating procedure; the interviewer is building goodwill and *keeping you interested*. Don't cancel your other interviews. Even if you have a firm job offer, compare it against what other companies have to offer when you are just beginning your career.

Two important points about the job interview should be kept in mind. First, be sure to *ask* for the job at the close of the interview. Second, when asked about salary, indicate a reasonable salary that is in line with the position. If you have done your homework, you should have a figure in mind before the interview.

YOU'RE HIRED!

You have done it right! You have chosen a career with a good future that, from all indications, will be satisfying to you. You have researched your career choice carefully. You have prepared yourself for a competitive market. Bet on yourself to win!

CONTINUING YOUR CAREER

You probably will repeat the career planning process described in this book several times. In fact, most people change their jobs at least five or six times during their lifetime.

Coupled with and affecting your career decisions are other important decisions you make about your life. These decisions can include the kinds of relationships you have with other people—getting married, having a family of your own, taking responsibility for your parents, developing new friendships, or maintaining old friendships. Decisions may center on how you spend your leisure time. You may wish to join community, recreational, or religious organizations.

You may wish to participate in the professional organizations in your field. These organizations can provide you with information about the current trends affecting your career. Some publish periodicals and provide job referrals, resource and information banks, and networking opportunities. Some offer annual conventions, special conferences, or specialized training.

Continuing education probably will be part of your professional development. Whether you wish to learn may not be a choice. Most individuals' careers change as a result of environmental changes. The organizations in which you work probably will change in some way. By being informed, you can anticipate these changes in your career and make decisions for yourself.

You may wish to review your short-range and long-range goals annually. You may find the career information and career planning process presented in this book helpful in future planning. Remember to be flexible, but not so flexible that you have no focus. Good luck!